Poetry Ireland REVIEW 80

Eagarthóir/Editor

PETER SIRR

Poetry Ireland Ltd/Éigse Éireann Teo gratefully acknowledges the assistance of
The Arts Council/An Chomhairle Ealaíon and the Arts Council of Northern Ireland.

Poetry Ireland invites individuals and commercial organisations to become
Friends of Poetry Ireland. For more details please contact:

Poetry Ireland Friends Scheme
Poetry Ireland
120 St Stephen's Green
Dublin 2
Ireland

or telephone +353 1 4789974; e-mail management@poetryireland.ie

PATRONS:
Joan and Joe McBreen

CORPORATE FRIENDS:
Bank of Ireland Arts Centre
ColourBooks Ltd
McEvoy Partners
Plus Print Ltd

Poetry Ireland Review is published quarterly by Poetry Ireland Ltd. The Editor enjoys
complete autonomy in the choice of material published. The contents of this publication
should not be taken to reflect either the views or the policy of the publishers.

ISBN: 1-902121-18-X
ISSN: 0332-2998

ASSISTANT EDITOR: Paul Lenehan
DESIGN: Alastair Keady (www.hexhibit.com)

Printed in Ireland by **ColourBooks Ltd** Baldoyle Industrial Estate Dublin 13

Contents
Poetry Ireland REVIEW 80

Feature on Vittorio Sereni

Eugenio Montale

THE LEMONS

Listen, the prize poets stroll
only among the trees
with uncommon names:
boxwood, privet, acanthus.
Me, I love roads that run out
among grassy ditches into
mud-puddles where kids
hunt skinny eels; lanes
that follow field-banks down
through beds of reeds and
end up in back gardens
among the lemon trees.

Best if the birds' chatter-prattle
is hushed, swallowed up
by the blue: then you'll hear
– clearer in the still air – the whisper
of companionable branches,
and catch a sense of that smell
that can't tear itself from earth,
drenching you in edgy pleasure.
Here, by some miracle, the battle
between one distracting passion
and another dies down, and here
even we who are poor
pick up our share of wealth –
and it's the scent of lemons.

Look, in these silences
which things sink into
and seem on the verge of
opening their closest secret,
you'd expect once in a while
to uncover some mistake
in nature, the world's still point,
some weak link, the loose thread
that leads us at last
to the heart of truth. Eyes

Brilliant example of a good nature poem

NB
Run on lines winding sentences reflect the progression of roads, activity etc.

rummage in every corner:
the mind seeks agrees argues
with itself in this perfume
that floats – as day fades –
over everything; a silence
in which, in every dwindling
human shadow, a troubled
divinity could be seen.

But the image fades, and time
takes us back to the din of cities
where you see the sky only
in bits and pieces, off up
among the chimneys. Rain then
wears the earth out, dreary winter
settles down around the houses,
light grows miserly, the soul bitter,
till one day, through a half-
shut gate, you see
among the trees in someone's yard
the yellows of lemons –
and the heart's ice melts,
and with their music
the golden trumpets of sunshine
blow your bones wide open.

– Translated by **Eamon Grennan**

Eugenio Montale

THE EEL

Eel –
cold seas' siren
that leaves the Baltic
for our warmer waters
our estuaries and rivers
and leaps from the deep
beneath the raging flood
and rushes up
river-branch to river-branch
one hair-thin tributary
to another
then farther in
deeper and deeper in
to the very core of stone –
seeping between
channels of mud and mire
until one day
a blaze of light
fired from the chestnut trees
ignites the flickerflash of her
in pools of standing water
and rivulets that spill
off the high Apennines
into Romagna: eel –
torch arrow whip
of earthly love –
whom our dikes alone
or those dried-out creeks
sliding down sides of the Pyrenees
lead back to Edens
seething with fruit and flower:
green spirit seeking life
where nothing bites
but parched earth and plains
of desolation: spark
that says everything starts
when everything seems charcoal –
a gnarled old

I like the shape of it.

buried woodstump: this
quick rainbow   flitting iris   twin
to the one under your eyelashes
(that flawless light you shine
among the sons of man
mudded in your ooze)
can't you see
she's your
sister?

– Translated by **Eamon Grennan**

Eamon Grennan

PATIENCE

When a heron, that protected bird, and a windhovering hawk
    appear
Framed in the one window for a minute, as the bigger slowly flaps
Towards Tully Mountain and the other does its Nijinsky trick of
    standing
On air – wings so fast they're like a long sentence out of Beckett,
    energy
Immensely expended on going nowhere, shaping up for the kill – I
    don't

Only remember the heron folding and unfolding itself over Omey
    Strand
When we spread your mother's ashes on the water and I said *an
    image
Of eternity* (though *patience* must be what I meant), but think also
Of the small heart hiding in heather-tufts and hoping – breath by
    breath,
Smell by smell – for another instant free of those lethal eyes, then
    another.

oochh...
like the ending
and I don't know
why

Michael O'Loughlin

MESSIAH OF MANHATTAN

The Jewish girls in the library of the Theological Seminary
Have the new-hatched look of nuns, their legs
Are naked and pale and flash like fishes' flanks
When they cross them, perched on high stools
As they scroll through time on their screens,
Pilots of a ship landed here at the top of the island.
Below us the rest of Manhattan steams, limping
Into its posthumous existence, muted, shorn, strangely diminished.

Up here, there is the sound of fountains without water
As the light floods through the huge windows. In the elevator,
A girl with old-fashioned hair smiles at me,
Like a messenger from the future. Surfacing,
I zoom up to the fifth floor, Rare Books section
To meet the grim Dutch prose of Pastor Thomas Coenen.
With gloved hands, a bad-tempered Russian hands me his book
One of twenty-six printed in old Amsterdam
In Sixteen Sixty-Nine of the Xtian era.   *Don't like hard to pronance words – breaks flav*
While Pieter Stuyvesant was milking his cows
In the green fields of New Amsterdam, Thomas was herding
human souls in the New York Babel of Smyrna, where
he saw the False Messiah Sabbatei Sevi with his own elected eyes
And wrote a sober account for his masters,
The Dutch East India Trading Company, assuring them
That Time had not yet Ended. They trusted no Messiah
But the hard gold in their purses and the cold storm
In their Churches, not even the wave
Which carries this brittle book to my hand,
Floating above the wrecks of a thousand ships
And half a dozen Temples.

Down at 42nd Street, the shuttle weaves
Back and forth to Grand Central Station
Till its steel wears out or the people have left, the people
Who paint angels on the fire house walls, but

I can tell them, there are no living gods here.
I know the waters will douse the phoenix's ashes
Because down at Ground Zero, we saw the seawall exposed,
Holding back the ocean, like the gills of a great fish.

- love the intro
- library, the people
- The story of the Messiah
  fitted great - really true
  to an' experience lived
- feel like he wrote it that day

Virgil

from THE GEORGICS, BOOK II (458-542)

If they but knew! They're steeped in luck, country people,
being far removed from grinds of war, where earth that's just
showers them with all that they could ever ask for.
So what if he hasn't a mansion with gates designed to impress
and callers traipsing in and out all morning long.
So what if there isn't a crowd gawking at the entrance with its
    gaudy tortoise-shell veneer,
and tapestries with gold filigree, and bronzes plundered on a march
    to Corinth.
So what if their wool's merely bleached and not stained with
    Assyrian dyes,
and the olive oil they use hasn't been diluted with that tint of
    cinnamon –
no, what they have is the quiet life – carefree and no deceit –
and wealth untold – their ease among cornucopiae,
with grottoes, pools of running water and valleys cool even in
    warm weather,
the soothing sounds of cattle and sweet snoozes in the shade.
There are glades and greenwoods, lairs of game,
young men wed to meagre fare but born and built for work.
Here, too, is reverence for god and holy fathers, and it was here
that Justice left her final footprints as she was taking leave of earth.
    And as for me, my most ardent wish is that sweet Poetry,
whose devotee I am, smitten as I've been with such commitment,
would open up to me the courses of the stars in heaven,
the multiple eclipses of the sun and phases of the moon,
whence come earthquakes, which are the reason deep seas surge
to burst their bounds before receding peacefully,
and are the why winter suns dash to dip themselves into the ocean
and are what causes the long nights to last and linger.
But if I am not the one to sound the ways of the world
because my heart's lack of feeling stands in the way,
then let me be satisfied with rural beauty, streams bustling through
    the glens;
let me love woods and running water – though I'll have failed. Oh,
    for the open countryside
along the Spercheus, or the mountains of Taygetus, its slew of
    Spartan maidens
ripe for the picking! Oh, for the one who'd lay me down to rest

in cool valleys of the Haemus range and mind me in the shade of
    mighty branches!
  That man has all the luck who can understand what makes the
    world
tick, who has crushed underfoot his fears about
what's laid out in store for him and stilled the roar of Hell's esurient
    river.
Indeed he's blessed, who's comfortable with country gods –
Pan and old Silvanus, and the sorority of nymphs.
High public office doesn't turn his head, nor regal pomp,
nor civil strife when friends and allies are at odds,
nor the Dacian league descending from the Danube,
nor even all concerns and cares of Rome, or any one provisional
    domain.
For those with wants he feels a sorrow, not envy for the ones with
    none.
The fruit on trees, all the country offers for the taking,
he'll gather. To cruel codes of law, or madding market places,
or the public record office – he simply gives no thought.
  Others rush in rowboats into uncharted waters, and race to take up
arms, they work their way into the inner courts and chambers of
    the king.

This man aspires to the sack of Rome itself, all its poor hearths and
    homes,
just so he might imbibe from cups inlaid with gems and sleep beneath
    the coverings of an Emperor.
That man stockpiles a fortune while he broods on buried treasure.
This man looks on with open mouth at speakers in the forum,
    while that one is struck dumb
by the applause that punctuates the talk of senators, and even
    common people,
and ripples all the way along the benches, while others still spill
    their brothers' blood
and ne'er a care. They strike out from the home place and forge a
    life in exile,
searching for warm welcome in a fatherland beneath a foreign sun.
  A countryman cleaves earth with his crooked plow. Such is the
    labour
of his life. So he sustains his native land and those who follow
in his footsteps; so he supports a team of oxen and keeps cattle in
    good order.
All go and no let up – so that the seasons teem with fruit,

fields fill up with bullocks, and big arms of barley stand in stooks.
They've overflowed the furrows, they'll burst the barns.
Come winter, and the best of olives run spilling from the mills,
the pigs come back aglow on feeds of acorns, the arbutus tree
refreshes its pale foliage – and in such ways the autumn serves its
    bounty,
while high on lighter ground the vintage basks on boulders and
     ripens in the sun's caress.
  And all the while dear sons await each show of his affection,
his home remains a model of propriety, with milkers plunging
their four quarters, and kids delighting in lush pastures
and locking horns in playful jousts.
The countryman observes his holidays by taking ease out in the fields
with friends around a fire, garlands adorning goblets
from which they'll drink to you, Bacchus, as he arranges contests
    and competitions
for the hired help, throwing javelins at a target marked on an elm,
and sturdy hands undress themselves for wrestling bouts.
That was the life, and those the ways the Sabines cultivated in the
    days of old,
they, and Remus and his brother, so there could be no doubt
that Tuscany would go from strength to strength and Rome become
gem of the world, embracing seven hills inside a single wall.
In days before a Cretan king held sway, times
when sacrilegious races fed on sacrificial oxen,
that was the life enjoyed on earth by splendid Saturn,
when they were yet to hear the flare of battle trumpets
and the battering of swords on an anvil.
But we have covered vast tracts of matter and, besides,
it's high time that we released the sweating horses from their halters.

                – Translated by **Peter Fallon**

Deborah Tyler-Bennett

LEAVING THE CITY

always complicates things. Especially when Dublin
strains wrists cloudwards after a short kip,
blinking as newsmen, sandwich-boards, and jarveys
stamp its thinning face.
Blinds down at *The Zanzibar*, *Pravda*, and *The Winding Stair*,
peonies trundled in bucket-loads past reluctant mares.
Already, storms brewing between an early-riser
and window washer (she booming where he's not
to put his ladder).

Going's tug, just as it all starts,
coffee brewed for Americans rocketed through
five cities in five days, O'Connell winos feeling sides
to check they're still all there, hawking spittle
at the sluicing Liffey.

Feeling the plane's seat below my haunches, *— under used word*
already set reluctantly for home.

Alma Carey-Zúñiga

She is dancing on the head of a pin.
Cuba Aereo. A twelve-cent mulatta
with almond eyes and dusty lace,
a tiara of five corals and red light,
coppers, paste diamonds,
and the foil of our charity.
She is washed in milk,
spinning in a sky gone the colour of lavender,
gone the taste of honey. She says:
you call me the colour of mule-skin.
She says: you call me Maria, *y me llamo Sofía.*
She says: you never listen – 'til I throw her down,
and read what she has brought:
'*...we are two days from Habana by foot.*
There is no trail and even with five mules to carry our gear,
we are hopeless. The trees rope us in, the hills echo gunfire,
and we do not know where to turn...'

Vona Groarke

WINDMILL HYMNS

In the shadow of the windmill, we put down our lives.
Something about its girth and ballast, the sun on its back,
the shiftless, amber absolute of it, foreclosed on other options.
We put down our lives as if for a moment – a break for tea
or to deal with an enquiry in the yard – and something about

its dereliction shut down at once on the chance of things
ever picking up again. Now, seven years on, this is us
finding the storeys equal to our time and too ornamental.
Even its decay does not refuse the compliment of sunshine,
the way the moon rubs up against it, or clouds distract

themselves upon its brim. What we were after then was a stopgap
for the lives we thought we'd live, that wouldn't be banked
in small-talk, disappointments, lack of cash; the intended,
blue-sky lives that would have us tilting at an evening do,
with arms like French film-stars and mouthfuls of moonlight

to slip us downstream into bed. That was then. I lie. It never was.
This instead is the relief of getting nowhere, of knowing
from the start how it must end. The same momentum,
self-same pace that drags itself and all its consequence
over the bones of another rattled year. I suppose, at some point,

it will stop, and all the shunt and grind of the day-to-day
come creaking towards another new conclusion, a new plan:
the last sacks loaded, the carts dismissed, handshakes,
gates pulled shut from the outside and then a silence
gaining on the sails, settling there, the way birds do, and the air,

the damp, the mould will all do now. How long before the wood
lets itself down on willowherb that finds itself at bay in shuttered
    light;
before the doors give up the ghost; the floors shrug the way
    windows
cannot bring themselves to do, until local lads with slingshots
and deadeyes see to them? How long until the ivy takes a hold

and starlings, like quicksilver, like silverfish, like a fastness
of silver spilled out on the stones? And us? We don't move.
Our way of holding on, of saying, *we've stayed too long*,
is like the way the children have of stopping play
to stand stock-still under the whir of starlings' hide-and-seek.

That what's missing should be called 'the coping' makes me
want to lay my face against the stone; let ivy root in my teeth;
weather grout my skin, my eyes take on the evening and its down.
Let my children stand within an inch of my life, so the way
their breath aspires could be the sky, or something close, to me.

Vona Groarke

TERMS AND CONDITIONS

Yet the burnt poet loves the fire
— Louis MacNeice

Back into a familiar room, see what you know,
as though you yourself had pulled the thing together
with the drawstring certainty of anything you ever turned
your hand to. But not here, where this room is busy
being someplace else. The pattern on the sofa's wearing thin.
The rug also is withering and even the view is slinking off

to brighter sights elsewhere. Put down your hand
as though from an instrument when the music gives itself up.
What is there? Perhaps a book, an opened envelope, or a box
of safety matches on the desk. You choose. Someone has set
a fire although the window is open so the book becomes
a commentary on what's happening to the room.

You know it. All the words inside are inscribed
on your memory, the way your imprint is upon this place.
The air is stranded when you so much as lift your hand
and every incremental word that marks a place out for itself
is discernible, if you could only see it, reach inside.
But your line of vision sags against the window

and you hear again the voice that says *all this could be yours*.
It echoes like a debt collector's bell, making even the pink roses
hold their breath, and you're not moving now. Not a whisper.
The book recalls its weight. The envelope addresses itself
again to someone else. The fire is set to warm to another hand.
Even the roses are borrowed from someone else's poem.

Aidan Rooney

MAY ALTAR

> i.m. Clare Rooney, whose mortal remains were found beneath a
> statue of the Blessed Virgin Mary, Holy Thursday 2000

I. *The Visit*

> e la domanda che tu lasci è anch'essa
> un gesto tuo, all 'ombra delle croci
> — Montale

Last night you were living with the neighbours.
They showed up with their boys as they always do,
on the porch some weekend evening, bearing a salad,
a bottle of red, a six-pack for themselves, and you

fell right in after them, no introductions, wearing
one of your flowered summer skirts and carrying
the big cream, ceramic bowl you started bread in.
Everyone smiled and kissed hello and acted normal

except for you, a certain coolness in your manner
as if to show some hurt that you hadn't been invited.
The seared tuna came out perfect on the new grill.
The kids behaved. I expected you to scold us

for the fuss, no call for half of it, the new kitchen
you escaped to while we sat down to food. 'There's
a pretty little girl from Omagh in the County of Tyrone,'
I overheard you sing, and when you left with them

you left with me a wheaten loaf with the deep cross
you liked to score on top, your white fingers disappearing
to tell beads in your apron pocket, your lips going through
the little motions of well-meant, recurring prayers,

the core of the bread, underneath, burning my palm.

II. *Lost*

A wind was in the room when the man woke
knowing he would never know how to die.
There was nowhere really left to hide but back
at being a boy in some secluded sun-warmed spot,
a place to spread the rug, lie down, a flat patch
in an unmown field, a dune in a summer seaside place,
repose he hoped his mother's eyes had found,
in extremis, before they had to seal them shut
on truths she must have come to know, so long
in silence and alone. 'Stop going through the rooms,'
he cried, 'and lie down dead.' But still she walked,
puzzled in familiar places, looking for children,
sensible shoes, a coat to go out in and get them,
wearing on her face the furthest thing from peace.

III. *May Altar*

Because you'd be disappointed
that Our Lady got no mention
in the various speculations
about your final, disjointed
movements, let me soothe that tension

and have in a vase appointed
budding lilies from your garden
to open for your assumption
in a place you'll find anointed
with blue, perpetual blossom.

IV. *Night Scent*

Not wide enough to pass the mower through,
a crevice in the ledge seemed ideal
for raising herbs. Crawling with weeds, a yew
that hadn't thrived, we exhumed all the soil

and filled the spot with a loamy, black manure,
glistening promise as it fell from the slit
in the plastic. Last night a woman lay there,
crushing profusions of lavender and mint.

Since she looked like no one I knew, I breathed
relief. A cool fragrance of pot pourri
slipped in through the window's gauze, bequeathed
to pause in the bedroom dark, to bring you back to me.

V. *The Shoes*

In the sightings she's seen as always going,
Mick, the Monday morning, to mass in St Joseph's,
John, who'd give her a lift in the rain, the same
that chilly Tuesday. 'She was awful fit,'
he says, 'All go. And sure she'd lay into you
if you stopped at all.' Tuesday evening,
shortly after six, a man from Tyholland
saw her going in the road. 'You could tell
she wasn't right,' he reported. She must
have turned to try and make it back to home
where she wouldn't be seen in such a state,
the coat that wasn't on all the way dropped
on the sitting-room floor beside the shoes
she must have slipped out of and laid aside.

VI. *Unfinished Nefertiti*

> *Dynasty 18, reign of Akhenaten, 1353-1336 BC, Quartzite,*
> *Egyptian Museum, Cairo, JE 45547, most likely the work of*
> *the royal sculptor, Thutmose*

A clasp might fashion hair clamps shut your head. 'Extracted
for further tests,' the coroner whispers, as I finger and let fall

new-washed curls I haven't felt in years. An amethyst bruise
the side you lay on is turning white. And your mouth is off.

It wears a puss, a kind of collapse I want to set right. Everything
is wrong. Nothing overstated. Outside the heavy double doors,

the attendant with the key cups his smoke against the drizzle.
Next door, like Thutmose in his workshop, the undertaker fires

faience for the famous other bust of you – Miss Omagh, 1948 –
while I wait in the County morgue with your exquisite head,

vacated and tenoned for hat or crown, my short vigil over
your polished face, prepared for inlays of glass, not enough

to find and bring you back to beauty, or send you forth complete.

VII. *Statue*

I will take and leave it. The house is as good
as empty, and less she'd want to come with me
than stand here in the rain, watch over you,
and *pray for us who have recourse to thee.*

Fergus Allen

IN THE HOTEL

Round the corner from the passenger lift
The goods lift waited with its door wide open
While two blue-jeaned removal men attempted
To shift a bulky something in or out.
Whatever it was, it was tightly wrapped,
But metallic corners and knobs protruded,
Catching the lintel at each push or heave
Or getting themselves wedged between the jambs.
When tilted, loose parts slid about inside,
And a sickening odour filled the lobby.

Damage having been done, the men revolted
And crashed the thing slantwise into the lift,
Where its impact quivered the chandelier
And alarmed the guests, all of whom then peered
Into the cage, to see what lay there, static,
Its doors wide open – with a human body
Visible face down among foreign rugs.
It fell to the police to turn him over
And show the shabby clothes, the black moustache,
The eyes closed down into a sallow face.

His papers were beyond us, words unreadable,
In a tongue officially known as hard.
Then we were told to leave, and plastic tape
Marked off what was called the 'incident area.'
But the face remained with us, like a haunting,
As of a being with a mask not ready
To revert to the state of lifeless matter,
Saying, hang on, I've yet to make my point –
But emblematic of a man misled
(As we all of us find ourselves misled).

Fergus Allen

OUIJA

If the evidence is to be trusted
'Barnaby Wishford' presents himself
each time the aging friends get together
to raise a moistened forefinger cautiously
into the gale of the spirit world.

There is no billowing-out of curtains,
the flame of the night-light doesn't tremble,
the Cuban mahogany is steady.
The Ouija, though, has its hesitations,
trying to choose this letter or that.

Does uncertainty rise from the furniture
or is it a bias of the brains
where these open minds are bottled up?
Now the pointer shoots across the table,
moves once more to 'B,' and then to 'A,'

as it did last week, spells it all out
and pauses. U.N.H.A.P.P.Y., it says next;
but when questioned just repeats the name.
What are Cyril, Liz and Seán to do?
What entity has them in its sights?

Keep well clear of it, warn the advisers,
you will learn the secrets in your time,
when the other driver's claim for damages
has been thrown out of court and the crowd
has strolled away from the crematorium.

Gavin Selerie

from *Le Fanu's Ghost*

Author's Note: *Le Fanu's Ghost* is a work in progress dealing with the Le Fanu, Sheridan and Blackwood families, all intertwined by marriage. It is partly a Gothic work and in other ways an exploration of Irish culture.

NORTON VERSUS NORTON

My dear Carry, I have no humbug.
At Great George Street, when I saw you
dance an exhibition quadrille, you had
a good measure of *ton*, and I'd loved you
several years, a black pearl, a lily
to spiflicate a man alone in chambers

But like your country-folk you lack
the bridle-rein. Pardon me,
the lady now bearing my name
is a mark for the talkers
uncorseted on her blue satin sofa—
the *Arabian Nights* in person—
when a man holds her hand
longer than necessary

This Londonizing keeps a tongue keen,
I know, and talk is sharp sauce
to the palates of men. There's an income
from your scribbling—we needs must
scrape to come off right

How dare you lecture me:
A man must be allowed to smoke
and not just in his den

Your endless letters, your flock of friends,
your family with its history—
can't endear even a Greek profile
to the Grantley sort

Twenty minutes behind the dinner hour
and r-r-really fearing it is late
you lower your eyes, look up from your lashes
mistress of whatever part
spells damage, a hundred variations
yet all one way

You think in flashes and dream
like *the harp that once...* (I cannot remember).
Your cleverness tears the face
from our house

You speak of what is due.
A woman is a mute in these things:
the money has fallen in and been replaced,
that's all. Capital, whereat you aim
your superbest sneer, has its instant duties

A husband can retain your *paraphernalia*—
jewels, books and clothes

There may be latent love like latent heat
in the midst of coldness

If I trespassed—touched your papers
with my cigar, flung my law books
across the room—let it be the lapse
of an anxious spirit, wanting to hold
his own on a shifting stage

I hope, and *think*, you will understand
these proceedings

      Your poor worn out Georgie
      Recorder & Magistrate

Dear George, Call me enigma: I am that
to myself. What is alleged (if it be alleged)
is a blank in some gnome's eye

What was not cannot be proved—
what if a maid saw me put my collar to rights,
what if I pencil and rouge?

You tore up my letters, poured brandy
over my writing book, struck your Lucifer match
to set the whole in a blaze.
You placed a scalding kettle on my hand,
left the room and said, *Brush the crumbs away.*
I went to the drawing room, locked the door
and you smashed it down.
I snatched the pipe from your mouth,
you squeezed my throat till I gasped for breath.
You said it would teach me to brave you
and yes sometimes I'd goad you
to get a response

You were mad to marry me at eighteen
and turned me out of the house
nine years after

My mother said, *You cannot always live at home*

We walked a dozen steps in dazed union
to hit upon crossways

You barred me from my boys—
dragged them round in a damp hack-cab,
locked them up because they appeared
at the play in a box with me,
had your servants bruise me as a cartwheel
when I found my way inside,
let me come only to see the youngest
a lead box inside another
of purple and velvet

A man purchases a wife as he would
buy a fine blood-mare or hound.
He may stamp or foam when there
is no dolly-dolly compliance

You scowl over bills already paid
hardly stirring like 'the late G—N'
noted at school, till the hiss of Mrs
prompts an action for *crim. con.*

In the fiction of ONE the Law
has me fast: neither apart nor together
I have no self and Grantley won't grant
how the Trapper sings

You subpoena my bank records and book contracts
digging for the *dis* of dishonour
but you have the proofs you suppose:
sometimes two short sentences
caught in a diorama

You searched into every corner
and never knew me

One might build up a respectable figure
in negatives: not to go out, not to notice,
not to laugh. But Irish blood *will* dance

My history is real—there's no poetry here to distract you.
You have the legal copy-right of my work
so—claim this

      Your affectionate
      Caroline

David Wheatley

TOUCHTONE

should you
        if you
                need
you suspect
         the ghost
                 of a breath
scarfing
      wreathing
              between
shoulder
        and neck
              insistent
finding you
        there
             with a word
in your ear
       asking
            should you
pressed to
       want to
            open
the cave
      of your ear
               that I trace
from behind
        my voice
            in the less
than breath
      of waiting
              desire
gaining
     closing
          on you
holding
     off
       until

if I press
      you too
           the waiting
cave
   of your ear
        receive
the word
     I speak
        scattered
to empty
    should you
        unless you
because we
     when we
        press now

David Wheatley

THESE EXPIRING VITALS

You know what I don't like? When we talk about poetry, that's what,
that stupid little self-satisfied word. It's a habit I must have fallen
into somehow, over the years, don't ask me how. Is this a poem? Is
this a political poem? What does it tell us about gender, persona
and language? Is this a *good* poem? Give a brief overview of the crit-
ical debate and its contexts. I was humming the Joni Mitchell song,
'This Flight Tonight,' from *Blue* as we skirted the coast from LA to
San Diego. It's funny how I could like that so much, and then go
and buy *Hejira* and listen to it once and never again. She must have
gone off all of a sudden or something. On the day, the conference
panellist spoke for twenty minutes, then fielded questions such as,
Am I in the right room? I'm glad you raised that point. My suit was
presentable, if cheap and visibly plucked. One time I left my name
tag behind in the coffee dock, but when I went back it was still
there, the waitress smiling as she handed it over. So how did she
know who I was without my name tag on? What is the context of
this context? Like I gave a shit. The blimp hung in the air and the
aircraft carrier hulked in the bay. There'd been some extreme weather
upstate, with mudslides and all, but we were just fine. What is the
writer trying to say in this passage? Does he succeed? The one thing
I will say is, I never bring enough socks when I travel. The cancella-
tion fee for the extra day was almost the same as the room charge,
how about that? I felt like staying just for the hell of it, to spite them.
To spite myself, really. So all in all the conference went well. Is this
a poem? Does the author employ symbolism? Give examples. This
is a laugh, isn't it? I mean, like I care about my so fucking superior
feelings anyway. If you're Wallace Stevens or something, go ahead
with your 'poem' this and 'poem' that, if you really must. But are
you? Are you? Some words we're better off just dropping altogether.
Some people don't know when to give up.

Myra Vennard

THE SAFE HOUSE

Things that fall
                    from another life:

a dream of children
with identical faces
and eyes of a different colour;

the single seagull
that draws me to the sea.

Sometimes to wake
is to visit
the portrait in the attic;

the sea that sinks
behind an unknown street.

Looking beyond the limits
my life snatches back from the land:
walking on water –
the safest place to be.

Mary O'Donnell

TATTOO

Sometimes you're a girl in boots
with blue tattoos on her thighs,
crossing the city northwards,
finding him in the long red car
where you murmur quietly,
leaning in the window,
the wind skinning your white arse,
blowing the pleats of a short,
short skirt in a fan around
your hips.
          Though his lips
try to shape themselves around
the script of your tattooed thighs,
truth is, neither you nor he
learnt to read hieroglyphs
when it would have been easy,
in the time of luscious hours,
when what you saw was suppressed,
those massed, ephemeral, butterfly-wings,
alive with colour, determined
to stir the space between your thighs.

oh Mary
what filth!

Mary O'Donnell

RETURN TO CLAY

It is not hard.
Go west or south, north,
east if you wish. Take
the swift path to the soil,
in boots or killer heels,
dungarees or velvet. The garments
are irrelevant, are merely
a beautiful counterpoint
to the moment when you sniff
the air and realise your pores
have filled with the smell of clay.
Let clay drive out all dangers
that prey on you at night.
If needs be, kneel down, speak
to the earth about your burden,
ask it to share the great weight
you cannot bear in solitude.
The earth will accept you.
It will not judge your frailty,
nor torment your weakness.
There is no shame in being tired,
or anguished, in feeling fear
when your ears are bursting
with the wrong sounds, when
your brain waves stridently
with fashioned ideas.
Let the earth hold you; be a child
again. If your mother never held
you, if your father could not touch you
without shrinking, speak to the earth.
Lean in close, feel the strong arms
of the old earth, that clay – powdered,
heavy, wet, wormed – feel what
knew your nature before you knew
yourself. Rest in the earth.
It is waiting.

Grim

Adrian Rice

THE APOLOGIST

Fine words from a man
From whom words came easily –
Drawn from his midnight mouth
Like a chain of silken scarves.

Biddy Jenkinson

RECORDING ANGELS

Máire Ní Mhurchú agus Diarmuid Breathnach, *Beathaisnéis 1983-2002* (An Clóchomhar Teoranta, Baile Átha Cliath, 2003), €18.

This is the eighth volume in a series which began with *Beathaisnéis a hAon*, published in 1986. In their editorial to the first volume, Máire Ní Mhurchú and Diarmuid Breathnach, librarians by profession, regretted the lack of a National Biography and outlined the task they had set themselves. They would celebrate the lives of those whose lives and works enabled Irish Ireland to survive. They would create a verdant graveyard where tenant, landlord, linguist, country man, jackeen, writer, scribe, revolutionary poet, maker of aislings, scholar, teacher, fascist, agnostic, catholic, protestant, dreamer, activist... would lie side by side. A grand post-mortem céilí of *Gaeilgeoirí*. Only the dead would be admitted.

They completed five volumes for the period 1882-1982, interviewing more than 800 people: friends, relations, descendants of their subjects, in addition to intensive ferreting in all available written / recorded sources. They added two more volumes, *forlíonadh*, for the periods 1782-1881 and 1560-1781, since it was not easy to shut the door on those who had died before 1882. *Beathaisnéis 1983-2002* is an *oighre neamhleithscéalach*, an essential sequel to the 1882-1982 volumes. More actors had qualified for inclusion.

I suspect that the editorial declaration in the introduction to the eighth volume *'Gan aon amhras sé seo an leabhar deiridh'* will be pushed aside by the pre-1560 and post-2002 dead, who will insist on having their bones arranged and their spirits restored by Diarmuid and Máire. The eight volumes are an *'éadach gan uaim,'* a seamless cloth that could serve as a banner for those of us who are still marching. We are no mean people and here is our history in all its richness, set down in the book by the two recording angels. They imagined it, not as a work of reference alone – though it is a reference book that the researcher will clutch to his / her heart before eating – but as an adventure story also. The angels are detectives in disguise and many of the entries are as intriguing as a case notebook. See, for example, the entry for Máire Ní Scolaí in this most recent *Beathaisnéis*, or glance at the speculation on page 245 as to the sex and identity of Anna Príor / Seón Anna Príor.

For the first time those interested in modern Irish literature, in Irish, have a handy traveller's guide. I took the 1560-1781 volume, *Beathaisnéis 7*, with me on a recent trip to Kerry. Until then I had often stopped in Muckross for coffee, unaware that three distinguished Kerry poets are buried in the Abbey. *Beathaisnéis* led me to the plaque that reads: \

> Seafraidh Ua Donnchadha, d'éag 1677
> Aodhagán Ó Rathghaile, d'éag 1728
> Eoghan Ruadh Ua Súilleabháin, d'éag 1784
> Piaras Feiritéar a crocadh, 1653
> Le linn ár ndaoirse, b'aoibhinn, cóir,
> gach éigeas díobh ag ríomhadh ceoil.

It was set there by an tAthair Pádraig Ó Duinnín (*Beathaisnéis* 3,4,7), whose dictionary is a joy to all who like words. I never reached my intended destination. Piaras Feiritéir had been hanged on Cnoch na gCaorach in Killarney according to *Beathaisnéis* 7, and it seemed necessary to set out for Killarney to look for his monument outside the courthouse. Reading *Beathaisnéis* has that effect. As Liam Ó Muirthile says '*Níl aon iontráil inti nach spreagann rud éigin...*' The same volume sent me on a pilgrimage to the Liberties, Dublin, where Tadhg and Seán Ó Neachtain were at the centre of a new departure in Irish poetry, prose and scholarship in the early eighteenth century. There is no memorial to them, or to any member of their school, in the area.

Beathaisnéis 1983-2002 is a loving inventory of those who were with us until recently. As it was going to press, Risteard Ó Glaisne died. The tone is not elegiac. There is an infectious delight in the richness and wonderful variety of the lives recorded. We see Daniel Anthony Binchy 1899-1989, who compiled the great six volume source for early Irish law, *Corpus Iuris Hibernici* (Institiúid Ard Léinn, 1978), riding his horse in the Phoenix Park and hunting with the Ward Union. We wonder if we would have Tomás de Bhaldraithe's *English-Irish Dictionary* if the young De Bhaldraithe, who went on a scholarship to the Sorbonne, École des Hautes Études in 1938, had not been forced to return to Ireland by the outbreak of war.

Here is Conleth Ellis 1937-1988, who was for many years chairman of the board of Éigse Éireann/Poetry Ireland. His five collections of poetry in Irish and five in English are listed 'Ní móide go bhfuil sé dleathach ar fad saothar Gaeilge Conleth Ellis a scaradh ón a shaothar Béarla.' Cathal Ó hÁinle. And here is Tomás Ó Floinn, 1910-1997, who in *Athbheo*, 1955 and *Athdhánta*, 1969 returned poems from the old and middle Irish periods to circulation in modern Irish.

Details catch at the imagination. Máirtín Ó Direáin's first two collections, *Coinnle Geala*, 1942 and *Dánta Aniar*, 1943 – of which Tomás Mac Símóin has said 'The publication of these early collections marked the birth of modernism in Irish Poetry' – were published at the author's expense. Due to a clerical error, Mícheál Ó hAirtnéid's birth certificate read Hartnett instead of Harnett. He decided to keep the 't' in the English version of his name since it was closer to the Irish. Dónal Mac

Diarmada, File Ghaoth Bearra 1889-1995, who wrote many popular songs, was a postman from 1906 till 1964 when he retired at the age of seventy-five. We are given his daily fifteen mile walk : ón Choimín síos bealach Mhín an Lábáin go Loch Barra; ó sin ar ais go Doire na nGriall, Doire na nAspal, Doire Sheanaigh, Doire na Coradh agus Abhainn na Marbh.

The authors remember Celtic scholars of all nations, politicians who influenced the fate of the language, folklorists, hymn writers, linguists, singers, journalists, musicians. Alan Titley in *The Irish Times*, 7 June 2003, said of Volume 8 'They (*na húdair*) have read, digested, understood, controlled, collated and made concise a massive amount of material from innumerable sources and have presented it with directness, clarity and style. This work is no less than a detailed history of Gaelic Ireland from the mid sixteenth to the late eighteenth century told through the lives of those who were there... The book is replete with intriguing connections and cross-references, and roads that lead us through the social and cultural history of the time.'

As the authors themselves said, 'Is suirbhé faoi cheilt é ar: chreideamh; oideachas; aicme; cúrsaí teanga (an cainteoir dúchais versus an breac-chainteoir versus an foghlaimeoir); rannpháirtíocht na gcontaetha; slite beatha; gnéas nó inscne...' *Beathaisnéis* stands alone at present but surely it will encourage others to undertake a similar work in different, though often overlapping, fields: Oglaigh 1916-1923; the Women's Movement; the Trade Union Movement; the Irish Theatre...

Those for whom Irish literature is something written in English in the last few hundred years, might, as a token exercise in open-mindedness, run their finger nails along the spines of these eight volumes. Within the Irish tradition those who preserve the record are revered. If we lose the past how can we appreciate the present or imagine the future?

As a tribute to the undertakers I would like to finish with a quotation from a poem by Seathrún Céitinn:

> Fágbhaidh Feart na Flatha Fíre
> Fúmsa tamall re tagra maoidhte.
> Dom is dleacht a leacht do líonadh,
> Dom is eol a sceol do scaoileadh,
> Dom is dual a ruaig do ríomhadh,
> ós dom is cóir a ghlóir do chaoineadh.

The literary partnership between Máire Ní Mhurchú and Diarmuid Breathnach has produced eight volumes over twenty years. Many of us look longingly at the pre-1560 period and hope that they will be tempted to explore in that direction next.

Ruairí Ó hUiginn

'OCH, A CHINN...'

*Dán Eimhire, bean Chú Chulainn ar fheiceáil chorp a fir di. Labhrann sí
le baill mharbha a fir ag cuimhniú ar an gcaoi a mbíodh siad agus
Cú Chulainn beo. Is dóigh gur san 15ú haois a cumadh an leagan áirithe
seo atá le fáil sa scéal Deargruathar Chonaill Chearnaigh; Tá leagan níos
sine (8ú haois?) ann i stíl dhoiléir roscach nár cuireadh in eagar fós.*

Och, a chinn, ón, och a chinn!
Cé gur meascadh tú ar an linn
Is iomaí slua dár thugais éag
Cé gur éag tú féin, a chinn.

Och, a shúil, ón, och a shúil!
Thugais domheanma dúinn;
Is ionann an t-ionad 'na mbeidh ár leacht,
Is ionann an uaigh a dhéanfar dúinn.

Och a airm, ón och a airm!
Is iomaí slua ar ar bhris tú maidhm;
Ní rabhais seachtain riamh,
Nach dtugtá bia do bhuíon

Och, a lámh, ón, och a lámh!
Do bhís seal go sámh;
Is minic a théiteá thart ar mo cheann
Och, b'ionúin liom an lámh.

Is maith liom, ón, is maith liom,
A Chú Chulainn chrua na mbeann,
Nár dheagaíos riamh do ghnúis
Is nach ndearnas drúis thar do cheann.

Ionúin an béal, ón ionúin an béal
Ba bhlasta é ag insint scéal;
Ó d'fhás gean ar do ghrua,
Níor dhiúltaigh tú trua ná tréan

Ionúin an rí, ón, ionúin an rí
Nár dhiúltaigh fós do dhuine ní
Deich lá fichead is anocht
Ó bhí mo chorp lena thaobh

Ionúin an fear, ón, ionúin an fear
A mharódh mórshlua gach seal
Is ionúin a fholt forórga fuar,
Is ionúin fós a ghrua geal

Ochón och ón, ochón och!
Is luaithe mé ná crann le sruth
Ó inniu ní fholcfaidh mé mo cheann
'S ní abród ní ar bith is fearr ná och!

John McAuliffe

INSIDE MY HEAD: THOM GUNN

Thom Gunn's first poem in his *Collected Poems* is 'The Wound.' One of
its subjects, perception and how our mind mediates the world, was a
continuing preoccupation. In the poem, the convalescent Gunn is
enthralled as he reads and relives Homer, till in the last verse there is a
joltingly Shakespeare-like stress on the word 'thought,' an indication that
for Gunn the true world in which we live is the imagination:

> But, when I thought, rage at his noble pain
> Flew to my head, and turning I could feel
> My wound break open wide. Over again
> I had to let those storm-lit valleys heal.

The poem relates how strongly reading affects its reader: a notable
feature of Gunn's work in its insistence that the poem should focus on
character, on the self who participates in the poem, and thereby involve
us as readers in the poem's action.

Gunn's poems are never happy to describe, to make us see the familiar
in a new way, or to estrange the mundane world. There is no fetishization
of the real and material world as an end in itself in these poems, and
Gunn never relaxes or tails off into litany. Instead the poems are sudden
and shift course quickly, often describing an action or a character or
cause and effect.

Gunn spoke and wrote often about how important W B Yeats was to
him: as an undergraduate, Yeats was hard to find in bookshops and was
not part of his education, so that when the Macmillan *Collected* eventually
came out in 1952 he absorbed and discovered the poems for himself. Yeats's
contrary influence echoes through all his books, in sequences like
Troubadour where he writes songs for a serial killer just as Yeats had written
songs for Crazy Jane, in the enjoyably caustic epigrams of 'Readings in
French' and *Boss Cupid*, the big stanza'd elegies (for individuals and a soci-
ety) of *The Man with Night Sweats*. This last book, which won the Forward
Prize in 1992, introduced Gunn as the documenter of AIDS and its ravages
among his friends, although alongside Gunn's elegies and laments are
celebrations of pre-AIDS life and the attractions of danger, as in 'In Time
of Plague' and 'Saturday Night' where, in the latter poem, he argues 'Our
Dionysian experiment / To build a city never dared before / Dies without
reaching to its full extent, / At least in the endeavour we translate / Our
common ecstasy to a brief ascent'; and records 'At length the baths catch
fire and then burn down, / And blackened beams dam up the bays of ash.'

It is Gunn's style and variety that makes each of his books so enjoyable and instructive. Thom Gunn loved to improvise. His early work gives the lie to the idea that form is not experimental, as he put it in an interview with Jim Powell:

> In looking for a rhyme, even in just mechanically trying all the conso-
> nants in turn on your suffix, you are exploring possibilities in your sub-
> ject...As you get more desperate, you actually start to think more deeply
> about the subject in hand so that rhyme turns out to be a method of
> thematic exploration.

It is easy to see how Gunn thrives on the questions that form asks in his early poems, like in the iambic pentameter of 'I know you know I know you know I know,' a refrain in 'Carnal Knowledge,' a poem from his first, undergraduate book *Fighting Terms* (1954). After he moved to the US with his lover Mike Kitay, he began to read and emulate American free verse. Unable initially to catch its rhythms, he used syllabics to wean himself off the more regular rhythms he'd used so inventively in his first books so that in 'Considering the Snail' and 'My Sad Captains' he plays delicate half-rhymes and formal diction off a seven syllable line, and succeeds in striking a new note in lines like 'but before they fade they stand / perfectly embodied, all / / the past lapping them like a / cloak of chaos. They were men... ' However, when Gunn goes over completely to the 'other side' the results are just as successful and intriguing, as in a later 1960s poem like 'Touch' where he writes,

> Meanwhile and slowly
> I feel a is it
> my own warmth surfacing or
> the ferment of your whole
> body that in darkness beneath
> the cover is stealing
> bit by bit to break
> down that chill

and a mid-70s poem like 'The Idea of Trust' which uses pauses and line-breaks to score the poems for an immediately effective and dramatic speaking voice and begins:

> The idea of trust, or,
> the thief. He
> was always around
> 'pretty Jim.'

Like a lilac bush or
a nice picture on the wall.

Character sketches like this recur in his later work, and seem to have been a way of ensuring that his poems never drifted into either argument or a too-lyrical remove from the social world.

Gunn's combination of lyricism and argument, of free and formal verse makes his *Collected Poems* a consistently enjoyable, interesting and instructive book. His subsequent, engaging last collection, *Boss Cupid*, elegises Robert Duncan and Donald Davie, two poets whose seemingly opposite styles are both related to Gunn's. Gunn knew the rarity of his own achievement and here he generously tries to find it in the work of others – the latter elegy praises Davie for the variety of his enthusiasms:

> That was what I admired about you
> your ability to regroup
> without cynicism, your love of poetry
> greater
> than your love of consistency.

In 'The Gas Poker,' a late poem about his mother's suicide, 'her release,' Gunn describes his and his brother's reaction when they discovered her body. This beautiful, sad poem throws light on the style and subject of much of his early, elegiac work and is another sign of the continuities in subject between the bereaved son and the San Franciscan. The last book's other poem about his mother, 'My Mother's Pride,' which lists her proverb-like advice to her son ends, typically, with the over-arching imaginative summation: 'I am made by her, and undone.' It is this ability to think about his subject, to risk statement as well as observation that makes Gunn such a necessary poet. Time and again, he brings readers up short by not bringing his poems up short, as in 'The Bed' which sets a scene and then moves away from it:

> We lie soft-caught, still now it's done,
>   Loose-twined across the bed
> Like wrestling statues; but it still goes on
>   Inside my head.

In his poems he was always as interested in style as its subject, which was usually his relation to and understanding of the world. That broad subject, the human world, discovered in him the restless enquiring styles which his readers enjoyed.

Thom Gunn, 1929-2004.

Ken Bolton

RECENT AUSTRALIAN POETRY

The New Australian Poetry, an anthology of 1979, edited by John Tranter, was consciously modelled after its namesake, Donald Allen's *New American Poetry* (of 1960) – for the good reason that it sought to mark the achievement of the revolution in Australian poetry that the American anthology had sparked. It was, in the parlance of the time, an 'active' anthology: not a survey of what was best but the advocacy of a certain group of tendencies and an attempt to announce that this movement had arrived and had a history. This latter function meant that, by the time of publication, some of the anthology's practitioners were already past the apex of their development and attainment. And, as with many active anthologies, some of what it presented was soon to be deemed dull, forced or whatever. But that numbers could be mustered was important for establishing the phenomenon's *bona fides*. The major names stood up well and, interestingly, much of the energy was in the tail: younger writers like Forbes and Duggan now seem, along with the editor, to be the major voices associated with the collection – at the expense of names that had got in on the ground floor, the actual 'generation of 68' as the publicity would have it.

This new poetry differed from that in the American anthology in being far narrower and more selective, as befits something coming after. The chief influences were the poetics (if not the actual style) of the Projectivists – Olson and Creeley – and the New York School – O'Hara, Ashbery, Koch and, increasingly, Ted Berrigan. The Beats had some attention but seemed to lack an aesthetic programme. Maybe Whalen was an influence, and Robert Duncan. The New York influence continued longer through subsequent Australian poets in this lineage. This is particularly true in Sydney. Two cities dominate Australian poetry, Sydney and Melbourne, an effect of population size.

As the poets have got older the best have continued to grow, and to grow more distinctly individual – so that description in terms of (American) 'open form,' free verse, ironic, urban cerebration (and celebration: 'I'm-in-love-with-the-modern-world' sort of thing, to quote Jonathan Richman), seem true enough but not to say a great deal about them. (The binary proposed in the 1970s was that of a new, more with-it, urban, American-derived poetic opposed to a more traditional range of forms and diction much attuned to a 'rural' Australia and Anglo-Australian values: Les Murray, A D Hope, Robert Gray, say. The polarization bracketed out many writers younger than Hope but older than Murray, who had been closer to the academic Americans, Berryman, Lowell, Roethke, and maybe Bishop.

The poets I discuss here are at the centre of this 'new' writing: John Tranter, Laurie Duggan, John Forbes, or they are related to it – in Pam Brown's case, an outsider (and not in the anthology) who has seemed to become central, as if supplying a missing term in the equation; or they are, at different distances, inheritors – Cath Kenneally, Cassie Lewis (or Peter Minter, Kate Lilley, Kate Fagan, Adam Aitken and others) – who might draw on the work of Forbes, Tranter and others, but draw as well on other aspects of new writing (subsequent US poetry, the different inflections wrought by 'theory' etc.)

In describing these poets to a new audience I feel I'm straying at one moment into hyperbole and another into understatement. The poets themselves will undoubtedly feel that I'm describing someone who is not quite them, or alternatively describing virtual über poets – manifesto versions of themselves – apparently able to work great but rather programmatically worthy feats. Discussing individual poems would be more to the point, but I don't think space allows.

John Forbes's work has been the most influential to date. This is attributable to a mixture of the vitality of his writing – a very heady intellection that is exhilarating to follow, possessing great verbal compression and wit – and his seeming to (willingly) typify the 'problem of the poet,' or of 'poetry.' This, and the high level of self-consciousness and criticality Forbes brought to bear on the 'idea' of Australia, and of Australia vis-à-vis the West, the Old World, Globalization, are central to his appeal. He observes closely a failing liberalism and failing Left, and remarks the diminished role of art, and poetry in particular, in a media-dominated and politically ill world.

Forbes routinely enacts a kind of dark comedy in relation to these themes and in relation to the idea of aesthetic routine itself; a double-edged and amusing mix of idealism and bad conscience, of optimism, foreboding and regret. In terms of influences the obvious ones behind him are Frank O'Hara, John Ashbery and Ted Berrigan. But they don't explain him. There is a curiously formal, Horatian quality, for one thing, and an air of scholasticism in the marshalling of categories. At the same time his work is invariably singled out as 'Australian' in its language and attitudes. Australian nervousness as to our 'status' – vis a vis the wider world, high or important culture, postcolonialism – is a central preoccupation for a few generations of Australian intellectuals and artists. Forbes torments the idea – when he is not energized by it.

Pam Brown's writing appeared on the radar in the mid 70s registering at first (from some illusory normative position) as 'on the margin.' Its mixture of anarchist attitude and enthusiasm for things as non-canonical as Tom Clark, Patti Smith, Jimi Hendrix, Rimbaud, Prevért and Woody Guthrie suggested mere radical-feminist, hip-left enthusiasm. A contender? But through the 70s and 80s her work continued to grow in density and authority and to gain strength from the diversity of its tap-roots into energy, ideology and critique outside the tiredly available central sources. Brown seems to have been 'coming from' (in one parlance) where others of necessity found they *had to be going* – towards a more fundamental critique of, and opposition to, the administered world of culture industry and suppressed conflict and the politics of the middle ground.

Brown's work has moved from the aphoristic, to chancing a manner more discursive, and in recent books, 50 – 50 and *Text thing*, to an amused, comfortless investigation of language and representation. The work is usually funny, amusing, but finally not-amused, very contemporary in feel, dealing with what we experience as a fractured, multiplicit cultural present. Brown's language is spare, always off-centre, jangly, halting and quick. The experience is of an eye, and of a voice that is not charmed by itself. A selected poems, *Dear Deliria*, is available in the UK from Salt. It has just – as I write – won the NSW Premier's Award for Poetry.

John Tranter has been the most culturally effective of what has some-times seemed to outsiders to be his own movement. The movement has refused to materialize, but in cultural mapping he is routinely posited as the counterposing term to that of Les Murray. Tranter's influence as poet has yet to surface strongly. It is partly that, outside parody (see Forbes's and Duggan's essays in his manner), he is not very imitable.

His work has some of the same themes, but is typically veiled and self-effacing, never seeming to speak directly in the poet's own voice. It tends to have its worries and ironies and perspectives on contemporary Australia and the contemporary world, yet to offer them as if in lieu of direct statement. The animus can usually be inferred, but not strictly attributed. Tranter's so far undisputed influence has been as anthologist and apologist for the new, and as publisher. His web magazine *Jacket* is one of the most read in the English language. His anthologies have been successful and have established reputations and written part of the history of contemporary Australian poetry. (*The Bloodaxe Anthology of Modern Australian Poetry* – published by Penguin in Australia – is available in the UK and Ireland. It is edited by John Tranter and Philip Mead). Tranter's major collections are eagerly awaited and read closely by a large number of Australian poets. Critics treat him unreservedly as major. Tranter's style is regularly re-tooled, re-invented, so that subsequent titles have tended to push previous high-water marks into the background. *Crying in Early Infancy* (one hundred sonnets) did this to the earlier *Alphabet Murders* and *Blast Area* volumes. *Under Berlin* seemed to move on again. Tranter's determined exercise in David Lynch-style schlock genre, *Floor Of Heaven*, was a further move. *At The Florida* seemed to ratchet up some gears further than *Under Berlin*. Currently Tranter's work is being promoted in the UK and internationally through volumes published by Salt. A study of Tranter's work edited by Cambridge writer Rod Mengham is due soon. It features among others a number of Australians of course, including poets Kate Lilley and Peter Minter, but also Americans Brian Henry and Stephen Burt, and UK authors Geoffrey Ward and Simon Perril.

There are constants in Tranter's poetry – a voice that is formidably impersonal yet familiar in tone and nearly always certain. It views a cosmopolitan contemporary West but a West viewed with the eye of an old-fashioned historian, a Gibbon, say. The perspectives drawn are long, the society is regarded with detachment and fatalism. For this reason Tranter's poetry seems stoical, bleak, or darkly comic. But the suspicion must be that – whether congenial or not – these things are adopted for their effects of authoritative finality of statement, of inevitability, and cliché. It's a kind of classicism – a vocabulary of signs, tones, gestures, *myth* in Roland Barthes's sense. The humour that underlies all this, that comes from it, is that we can enjoy what is offered at a surface level – and do, because the poems are entertaining – yet it is illusion, a perfection of form, a counterfeit so good but that we dare not cash it in. In a sense then the poems demonstrate form – or semiotics. The withdrawal of this so closely observed reality is signalled at the very surface level of the poems: humanist optimism is always undercut, denied, disappointed. If the poems are expressivist it is via the mechanism of presenting, as straw-men, replicas of what the poems do deal with: hidden behind that simulated disappointment at, say, the failure of love – or whatever - is … the failure of love? Or it may be that the overall falsity is offered as synechdoche for the specular real world and its unconsoling fictions?

Laurie Duggan has examined Australian history and its present through attention to public language, its demotic manifestations, and the manners of daily life. The personal is framed by and contrasted against this. His work has great humour, nearly always understated, and a sort of scrupulous accuracy both as to historical fact and the charting of mental life. Duggan's influences and orientation centred on American poetry (and general writing) on 'place,' on Beats like Whalen, and some English writing like that of Roy Fisher and Gael Turnbull – and further back Pound and Williams. His name used, for years, to be regularly paired with that of his friend John Forbes – probably to Duggan's disadvantage. But while Forbes was undeniably – and sometimes flashily – brilliant, Duggan's claim to serious attention can never have been in doubt. It now seems to me that Duggan, Forbes, Pam Brown and, say, Alan Wearne, may have supplied some of the best accounts of, and responses to, the last quarter of the twentieth century that Australia has produced. Duggan's early work loosened up and flowered into the booklength

Under The Weather, a poem of journal and process, geography and quasi-hippy doldrums and angst. It gained greater force and focus in *The Great Divide* – in which were poems that set out the parameters of much of his later endeavour: serious attention to politics and history as they unravel in the detail of everyday life and public lie. 'The New England Ode,' for example, stands as a corrective and riposte to much of Les Murray's enshrining of rural Australia. *The Ash Range* was an epic history poem looking at, and working with and recasting, documentary evidence from the settling of the Gippsland area of the state of Victoria. *Memorials* is again a book-length poem, elegiac in tone, farewelling Duggan's recent past: a youth lost gradually to age, and friends departed and departing. It returns to the style of *Under The Weather*, though by this stage Duggan's 'chops' as he might say, were better. 'Adventures In Paradise' (a tongue-in-cheek autobiographical poem telling the life of layabout young poet), his versions of Martial, and his many gnomic two and three-liners, are in Duggan's alternative, more purely satirical vein. They owe something, originally, to Ed Dorn's poetry of the late 70s. His recent *Mangroves* won the Victorian Premier's poetry award. A *New and Selected* is to be published in the UK by Shearsman publications. His poetry is capable of great reserve, devastating wit and intelligence, and a kind of goofing-off.

Cath Kenneally – a journalist, reviewer and, lately, novelist – first began publishing poetry in the 90s, making a late start. Her work moves within the parameters associated with the New Australian Poetry without her being a direct inheritor. It is the available style: open, free verse, sometimes using detail collaged together or otherwise juxtaposed, and examining of representations and of the fit of the private and public worlds. But, while the style might be regarded as 'available,' it is resisted enough by some critics still, her work attacked on occasion for lacking the more traditional beauties of regular verse. *Around Here*, her first large collection won the largest of the state poetry awards in Australia. Her second, *All Day, All Night* was published in the UK by Salt this year.

Cassie Lewis is a poet confessedly, but not obviously, indebted to John Forbes. She knew him as a poetry tutor and took a number of lessons to heart. The work is different from Forbes's but Lewis identifies qualities and desiderata in her writing attributable to him. Forbes has not always been a good influence on poets – a few have been too in his thrall and reduced to imitation and emulation. Lewis works a quite different territory. It is typically a poetry that seems impacted, tensed, and then to break forth from that bounded state with an assertive or declarative ener-gy. Its content is more avowedly emotional, its attention less focused on the discourse of power. Her work bears little relation, I think, to the US writing that helped Tranter's 'generation of 68' into being. Lewis lives now in America.

John Tranter

FIVE MODERN MYTHS

The Guarani Indians of Paraguay
like to keep a small cork loose in their dishwashers,
to 'introduce a spirit of lightness and unpredictability
into what is otherwise a repetitive activity,
and one tedious and unpleasant to contemplate
by the gods of the forest.'

In Kota Rendang, a small fishing village
on the East Coast of Malaysia, the wood carvers
refrain from spitting in front of the local cinema,
in case 'Clint Eastwood should become angry,
and blunt the edge of our blades.'

Until recently the fishermen of Muckle Roe,
in Scotland, used to scrub their decks with toothpaste
on the night of the Summer Solstice,
in order to placate the fish-goddess Fiona,
she 'of the gleaming teeth.'

The Mongolians of Ulaanbaatar have a great respect
for dwarfs, who are trained to recite poetry
in a sing-song voice in front of the television news
which is allowed to run silently in the background.
'A short rhyme contains the news,' is their motto;
using 'contains' in the sense of 'constrains,' or
'keeps within the bounds of propriety.'

The stockbrokers of Lakeville, Connecticut,
take care not to be seen mowing their lawns
on the thirteenth of the month, in case
a water spirit, the 'White Witch of Lakeville,'
should afflict them with cirrhosis of the liver.

– from *Studio Moon*, Salt, 2003.

John Tranter has published seventeen collections of poetry, including
Late Night Radio (Polygon, Edinburgh, 1998) and *Studio Moon* (Salt, 2003).
He has worked in publishing, teaching and radio production, and
currently lives in Sydney.

Pam Brown

ST EXPÉDIT

along route de Moufia,
uphill, past the chapel,
a man lies face down,
flat dead drunk
on the roadside –
white rum & zamal
or rum alone

black men
pace around
proclaiming
strife to the air,
haunted
by slavery

scrawny stray dogs,
wandering chickens
bark and crow
making a racket
through every night

voodoo turns
brother against brother –
rape and murder
in La Bretagne,
the ridge
across the next
rubbish-strewn ravine

please
send for the saint
as fast as possible

– from *eleven 747 poems*, Wild Honey Press, 2002.

Pam Brown, living in Sydney, is the author of many books of poetry and prose. Recent titles include *Drifting topoi* (Vagabond Press, 2000) and *Dear Deliria: New and Selected Poems*, published by Salt in 2003.

Chris Wallace-Crabbe

ON THAT ISLAND

Looking at how Mount Arthur eastward
had been lightly limned
           in a musky blue
he began to count the summers to come

reckoning on the fit brown ones
then the haggardly worn
           with a stoop and limp.
He ignored the dank tunnel following those.

Optimism he drank like a pure gold martini,
walking through blond nature
           and its choral turtledoves
beginning, as a rule, *in medias res*.

Dreaming was what he stored up anxiety for;
happiness came haphazardly,
           a bliss unbidden when
he followed Aphrodite's easy beaches, basking out.

To meander barelegged must mean turning back into
one of the frankly blest
or at least rattling good.

He thanked the twiggy land for his being in it.

Chris Wallace-Crabbe

ENDING WITH A PREPOSITION

The news could be hardly new while it becomes

fanatical and faintly luminous
but is life all that different or drear,
something more than a sticky wicket, when
you have let your sub to *The New Yorker* fall away?

Plenitude, the unseen flutefilled magpie
carolling its dulcet fanfaronnade,
pleases us, drawing the past to guarantee
a separateness in every living thing,

those lonesome ones constructing society
so as to get food, frock shops and police;
the rich woman's back fence now gone cutely mobile,
readier to say that this will end in tears.

The universe fills up with compensating cartoons,
more tousled cloud rolls in like tumbled blondes,
metaphysics falters yet again, and
extra cover is moved to backward point.

The sprained ankle is hardly where we're at.

Chris Wallace-Crabbe has published fourteen volumes of poetry, the
last being *Whirling* (Oxford Poets) in 1998, *For Crying Out Loud* (Oxford
Poets, 1999) and *By and Large* (Carcanet, 2001). He has received many
awards for his poetry. He was Director of the Australian Centre,
University of Melbourne, and is now Professor Emeritus in the Centre.

John Forbes

SPEED, A PASTORAL

it's fun to take speed
& stay up all night
not writing those reams of poetry
just thinking about is bad for you
                – instead your feelings
follow your career down the drain
& find they like it there
among an anthology of fine ideas, bound together
by a chemical in your blood
that lets you stare the TV in its vacant face
& cheer, consuming yourself like a mortgage
& when Keats come to dine, or Flaubert,
you can answer their purities
with our own less negative ones – for example
you know Dransfield's line, that once you become a junkie
you'll never want to be anything else?
           well, I think he died too soon,
as if he thought drugs were an old-fashioned teacher
& he was the teacher's pet, who just put up his hand
               & said quietly, 'Sir, sir'
          & heroin let him leave the room.

John Forbes

LESSONS FOR YOUNG POETS
   – *for Ramona Barry, Kieran Carroll and Cassie Lewis*

I

it's important to be major
but not to be
too cute about it – I mean
it's the empty future
you want to impress,
not just the people
who'll always be richer
& less talented than you.

2

'arbeit mach frei' translated
roughly by a nudist means
                          'an elevated tone
is no guarantee against pastiche.'

3

vacancy, impotence
& hysteria – that's your
best bet. after all, you
want to be craftsmanlike
don't you? for example,
try rewriting this –
'vacancy, impotence
& hysteria –
is that your best bet?'
Congratulations!
you've just improved

on the haiku form!

4

if you live in the suburbs
you can still write good poems

as long as you remember –
if he wasn't on the drinking car
he wasn't on the train!

5
(politics)

a) act as if
you can't believe
how lucky you are

b) learn how to spit
unselfconsciously

6
(love)

continually disappoint
the expectations of others,
this way you will come to hate yourself
& they will be charmed by your distress

7
Envoi

the rest is technical & you'll
steal it yourself
but just remember
if you take care of the art
                    your sister, Life
takes care of the human part.

'Speed, a Pastoral' and 'Lessons for Young Poets' reprinted with
permission from *Collected Poems*, revised edition, 2002, Brandl and
Schlesinger, PO Box 276 Rose Bay NSW 2029 Australia.
E-mail **book@brandl.com.au**

John Forbes was born in Melbourne in 1950, and lived for many years in
Sydney before moving back to Melbourne in 1989. He received many
prizes for his work and was widely published in Australia. He died
suddenly of a heart attack in January 1998. His *Collected Poems* is published
by Brandl and Schlesinger.

Thomas Shapcott

RECLAIM

My first visit to Limerick was the return
Avoided since my grandmother implanted the genes
And the restlessness. I spent my life
Being myself but in Boston or Chicago
They embraced me as cousin or family.
I spoke in an accent that was either smug
Or offensively Australian.

                                    Sing us your songs,
They said, or tell us your stories.
We all feel the hard soil of exile.
I felt anger.

                 No, I felt drawn in.
I was who I was and it had nothing to do
With them. Alone, I took bandages
Out of the waterfall that had appeared in the rainforest
I created archipelagos in the stones
worn out of unimaginable battles with friction
until shape imposed plans and consequences.

My life had been discovery and the truth
though it seemed everything was sudden
And unfamiliar. I sucked pebbles
As a comfort against thirst. Compost
Was the smell in my nostrils, real
As the treasuries or the Khazars,
Or all the vanished tribes.

                        I was a stranger
In my own land and inherited power,
That tool with the teeth of the dinosaur
Before change.

                    Listen, they said,
Listen to what you might be saying.
I grinned. I said I will sing a song.
There is no story like the lonely song
Of exile.

                    We hear your genes, they said.
Welcome.
                    The rocks in my mouth
Had grown as huge as volcanoes. Mountains
Were remembering rainforest
And the ancestral voices were as foreign
And as familiar as each part I sought to disown.

Thomas Shapcott was born in Ipswich, Queensland. A poet and novelist, he has won numerous awards including the Grace Leven Prize and the Myer Award. His publications include *Time on Fire* (1961), *Inwards to the Sun* (1969) and the novel *Hotel Bellevue* (1986)

Alison Croggon

THE WIND

I am done with everything but this business
of recalling what is human –
faint letterings in sand, this burning leaf
or a curtain blooming in a still room –
all I know of eternity. How it burns me,
how borderless I become in the wind

evaporating like the sweat of fingers
and blown blindly over the blind ocean –
no mark will tell the wind of my presence
my feet will fail to remember you
dancing in a dark room
o my love how the windows shudder

– from *Attempts at Being*, Salt, 2002

Alison Croggon writes poetry, prose, criticism and texts for theatre. Her books of poetry include *This is the Stone*, (Penguin Books Australia), *The Blue Gate* (Black Pepper Press) and *Mnemosyne* (Wild Honey Press).

Ken Bolton

TIMELESS MOMENT (LITTLE CUP SESTINA)

a true account of talking to a styrofoam cup, one night,
outside the university architecture department
— for David Saunders and Bruno Taut

little styrofoam cup
I really like you:
in my mind's idea.
That sort of
round, inflated look
astronauts have

in that pearly light they have
inevitably to get photographed in, cup,
a look
you take almost with you,
wherever you go, the look of
a thing to which illusions don't stick: the Idea

of the future as a rosy thing, the idea
that a sort of 1910 visionary German architect might have
had ('shining cities of
the night,' for example), little cup,
you don't support. You
look grubby no matter how clean you look.

The *look*
of shading, where you turn away from the light, cross-hatching
   can't suggest: the idea
of clean and dark as a continuum you
have at your shady edges, & have
in any light, is like a smudge! Little cup,
you were so resolutely the repository of

so many things you never wished to be the repository of.
Most of them negative (!) I *like* your look,
I think you are allright.   Cup,
Roland Barthes says: farce is the negation of the idea

of materialist hope (cf. Vico, Marx & others). Have
you heard of that? It is the notion, in your case, that you

repeat the idea represented by Cup (you
are one!), like farce repeats the idea of
tragedy – minus meaning, noble meaning. The idea the Bauhaus
   might have
had: about good design both *being*, & symbolising, The Future –
   you *look*
like you say nix to that. The idea
of you it is said, is degree zero, where zero means '32 below' –
   emotionally
         like 'cyronics for the brain,' not that I don't like you.
         What do you say, cup?

'I like you too – cup to human – you
have a clear idea of my status as replacement of
the Table and the Chair, as philosophical exemplars of reality, thru
   my *look*, real & artificial, & so reminding, comfortably, of
   Progress. Well I guess I don't remind of that, & that's what
   you're saying. You say, Don't worry but. And I like that.
   I'm useful too – did you forget? Probably you didn't.
   Maybe you should have a Coke out of me, if you have
   enough money. Do you have?'
'Stop there!' I said. 'Yes I do,' I said. 'I have.'

    – from *Selected Poems* 1975-1990, Penguin Books Australia, 1992.

Ken Bolton visited Dublin as winner of the James Joyce Foundation of
Australia's 'Suspended Sentence Award' for 2002. He attended the Cork
Experimental Poetries Conference in 2000. His most recent collection is
Untimely Meditations (Wakefield Press, 1997). His collection *At The Flash &
At The Baci* is forthcoming from Salt Publishing.

Jill Jones

SCREENS, JETS, HEAVEN

Lightning above the bay.
Sky night shimmers.
We almost scent rain.
Jet engines shudder on curfew
then cease.
Rain doesn't come.
The hills shape the clouds.
Blind stars – always.
By midnight they are covered
with the noise of our life.

We know heaven is vacant.
But on screen we are beautiful
in the pulse of the cables
dying in videos of memory –
our light in the dark frame,
the neon of a dirty world.

The midnight special
screens old rock and roll
a purity in its black and white moves.
So we find solace
when we peel back the covers.
We sing raw
but still beautiful
skimming the light from a song
wrecking harmony, sublime
and nonchalant.

Dawn sneaks us in, awakened.
A new wind is in from the south.
Out there the sea,
the new day's jets.

– from *Screens Jets Heaven: New and Selected Poems*, Salt, 2002

Jill Jones is a Sydney poet and writer. Her books include *The Mask and the Jagged Star* (1993), *The Book of Possibilities* (1997) and *Screen Jets Heaven: New and Selected Poems* (Salt, 2002).

Barra Ó Seaghdha

AMBIGUOUS BENEDICTIONS

Jill Jones, *Screen Jets Heaven: New and Selected Poems* (Salt, 2002), £9.95.
Kevin Hart, *Flame Tree: Selected Poems* (Bloodaxe Books, 2002), £9.95.
John Tranter, *Studio Moon* (Salt, 2003), £8.95.
Alison Croggon, *Attempts at Being* (Salt, 2002), £9.95.

> In their efforts to depict an Australian landscape our early painters,
> fresh from England, were perplexed by the trees: they were wrong
> in shape, gaunt and unkempt in appearance with unusual bronze or
> made melancholy by ringbarking... They saw with English eyes
> perceiving through English atmosphere illuminated with English light.
> A tyro can notice that in Talmage's picture of the 'Founding
> Ceremony in Sydney Cove' there is something amiss with the light.
> It is not Australian. So they painted scenes in an English manner, sub-
> consciously aware of their inadequacy.

These words are taken from 'Our Heritage in Australian Landscape,' the
essay by Roy H Goddard that introduced a 1952 volume, *Australian
Landscapes in Miniature*. This is the unavoidable question around which
Australian culture in the broadest sense has for long polarised. Does
Australia see itself as an ex-colony gradually raising itself from its tainted
origins towards the level of the mother country or does it affirm its own
identity, drawing hugely on its Protestant British heritage but also on its
Catholic Irish, Pacific and of course Aboriginal heritage? Though Australia
is having difficulty deciding this question at the level of national
institutions, allegiance and symbolism (as the virulence of the current
immigration debate suggests), the question has been largely answered in
the areas of literature and the other arts.

    It would be simplistic, however, to see Australian poetic history as a
journey from clenched pommydom, through the freer lyrical voice of
Judith Wright perhaps, on to the unabashedly Australian 'quality of
sprawl' associated with Les Murray and, in his own different generation
and style, John Kinsella.

> And over the flat earth of empty farms
> The monstrous continent of air floats back
> Coloured with rotting sunlight and the black,
> Bruised flesh of thunderstorms:

> Air arched, enormous, pounding the bony ridge,
> Ditches and hutches, with a drench of light,
> So huge, from such infinities of height,
> You walk on the sky's beach
>
> While even the dwindled hills are small and bare,
> As if, rebellious, buried, pitiful,
> Something below pushed up a knob of skull,
> Feeling its way to air.

Who would dismiss, even argue with this, the controlled formality of sound, syntax, rhyme and rhythm which opens out onto an awed apprehension of Australian landscape and light, in Kenneth Slessor's pre-World War II 'South Country'? The real freedom is the freedom to choose. The quality of the four books under review does not depend on the school of writing to which they could be seen as belonging, but on the completeness with which they establish a world in language. And in deciding whether this has been attained or not in a particular book, personal taste and affinity will have their say.

The personality that comes through Jill Jones's *Screens Jets Heaven: New and Selected Poems* is warm, open, humorous, democratic; a poem will often have its starting-point in everyday reality (a trapped insect, a casual question, an airport lounge, a tax form...) and then push towards a heightened awareness or realisation.

BALCONY

> The wood creaks and the iron rusts
> while we are talking
> and the western suburbs
> flow out beyond us under a Sunday sun
> and you wouldn't think if you were watching
> through the shattered glass of the phone-box on the corner
> that anything more important than life
> was crumbled about like flakes of croissant
> in the conversation
> that there was anything sweeter
> than the strawberry jam
> and a balcony breakfast
> and the whole neighbourhood listening.

The basic mode is one of celebration, though this seems harder won in the later poems, as in the close of the poem 'Rust':

You dreamt life, that sunny afternoon
a toast, a taste, a night ahead of
where you'd been, days in the chase.
Now the gravel crunches in the carpark
shiny random minerals – breaking.

A tide more obvious, there
over the sandhills. But still slipping by here.
Exposure. Recovery. Old lobster pots
coming to light
grappled with nylon, leaded hooks,
rust spun tide salt.

If it does not transform our idea of what a poem can do, if it is a little over-welcoming towards the muse's call, this is a poetry of honest appeal.

A generous-minded and very sociable friend used to introduce people from different walks of life to each other in almost heroic terms; unfortunately, conversation would prove difficult, as people struggled to live up to the introduction. Kevin Hart's publisher or blurb-writer risks creating a similar effect. The innocent reader may feel bludgeoned with praise. It is not enough that Harold Bloom should believe Hart to be 'the most outstanding Australian poet of his generation' and 'one of the major living poets in the English language' or that Charles Simic should describe him as 'one of the finest poets writing in English today'; we must also be told that he is 'a major figure in world poetry.'

Though Hart's poems are often grounded in everyday realities, they reach – through numerous evocations of light, space, sun, stone, wind, silence, birds and so on – towards a frankly religious or transcendental dimension. The convergence between the poetic impulse and the impulse towards prayer is relatively uncommon in a time when many poets make language their god or doubt its power to reach out into the world.

THOSE WHITE, ANCIENT BIRDS

And so they come, after the darkest month,
As though all guided by the one intelligence:
They play the air,
                    but cannot survive on light
Or feed upon the generous heat of day.

[...]

I do not think they know much about longing.
Those white, ancient birds,

                 they know just where to go
And fly there, at their appointed time,
Without a weighing up of gains and losses,

But I have no idea where to go,
And wait all morning by a window, the big sky blankly there,
Not knowing what I am waiting for
Yet aching for it just the same.

Any judgement of the success of Hart's poems may be influenced by the reader's own beliefs or aspirations. For this reader at least, the problem with the poems lies in the ease with which they lay claim to the spiritual. The clarity that strikes Harold Bloom as visionary comes across instead as just a little facile. This is how some poems conclude: '... as we made our way / Across the fields of sadness, walking towards the horizon'; 'All your future sorrows and your only blessing'; 'Where bread is broken / To make us whole, the inn of our desire'; 'And as though this other world would last, my love, I go to be with you.' The steadiness of tone and speed, the untroubled syntax, make this poetry less a spiritual experience than a leisurely stroll towards the infinite.

The 'Nineteen Songs' sequence from the 1991-1998 section poses further questions. To write poems when under the sway of erotic love is not unusual; but if the poems are offered to the world, they should offer more than a peek over the poet's shoulder: 'Sometimes you wake me up / When you are days away / In Tübingen or Bath / By entering my dream / With very little on: / Perhaps that new white bra / And those silk panties that / Ride up a little way...' One's unease at the ease with which the poet later slips into spiritual mode ('I think that truth is always clothed in love...) turns to positive distaste at the auto-benediction of the close: 'The shortest day will come / But God will look at us / And know himself at last: / And you will kiss his lips'

John Tranter is the leading poet of his generation; John Tranter is a leading contemporary poet; John Tranter is an important writer in mid-career: so the editorial matter of *Studio Moon* assures us in any case. This is a poet who does not pretend to be a voice of nature, or a conduit to the infinite; he is happy to show his own literariness. He offers in rapid succession a poem after Laforgue, a Chinese Poem, after Mark Ford, a version of Rimbaud, a response to a Veronica Forrest-Thomson poem, season poems in the Japanese *haibun* form, versions of Rilke, Baudelaire, Schiller, Max Jacob, Vicente Huidobro and a poem that uses the end-words of Matthew Arnold's *Dover Beach*. For one poet, the poem pays homage to the rose; for another, the only rose that matters is the rose-in-the-poem. While literary debate and practice sway to and fro, the poem of whatever kind demands a close encounter. What happens when we meet Tranter meeting Rilke?

> I hate this place. If I were to throw a fit, who
> among the seven thousand starlets in Hollywood
> would give a flying fuck? Or suppose some tired
> studio executive, taken by my boyish beauty – no,
> I'd suffocate. Charm is only makeup-deep,
> I reckon, and staring in the mirror too long
> can give you the horrors: that thing in the glass,
> it doesn't care.

This is fun to do, and fun to read the first time, but the unfortunate fact is that the Tranter poem all too often ends up looking like a pound-shop version of the poem it takes off from. It is easy to pick up the mannerisms of James Schuyler, Frank O'Hara and John Ashbery; less so, to catch the casual brilliance of their best work. And hasn't John Ashbery himself been imitating John Ashbery for far too long? It is important to insist on the difference between Tranter's clever but facile literariness and the kind of creative engagement with the work of other poets shown by another Australian writer, John A Scott, in his volume *Translation*.

Alison Croggon's *Attempts at Being* does not lend itself to summary: it contains theatrical texts of various kinds (none of which we are likely to see at the Abbey or the Gate), a kind of manifesto ('On lyric'), lengthy self-aware explorations of the writer's experience and the experience of writing, and poems of lyrical impulse, some fractured, some more immediately graspable. There is nothing tidy or comfortable about this book of 174 pages; there is no single route through the material. However, it is because, from the first lines of the first poem, the writer's attempts at being are so highly charged and carry such conviction that readers will respond with multiple attempts at reading. The completeness with which the writer's faith in the act of creative writing is tested and enacted in sound and rhythm and image induces trust in the reader. In the end, it may all come down to fifteen or twenty pages, but that is almost always the case with a book of poetry.

The shorter poems offer the easiest entry into Alison Croggon's world. 'Elegy' is surprisingly obvious, almost flat; there is something forced and over-wrought about 'Hands'; but then there is the deftness of a poem like 'Illness' :

Shadows move where thrushes pick
a few grains. The sky pours
ambiguous benediction. A derelict

fence sags under years
of vines. I am young
still, in this light that claws

furrows across the long
rebellious grass, this unhealed edge
of song.

If a certain old-fashioned earnestness breaks through in the long poem
'Amplitudes,' the books concluding sequence, 'Owl songs,' contains
writing that is dense, gnomic and very assured:

ash rose and rose of stone,
lymph and haemad martyred from the wood
undoing bone as paradise pricks sight –
the lovely cheek, the leaf, the tear, unfleshed
past wail or weal, flashed to shadow:
rose whose secret petals close the harm
blent for public pap into the fearsong:
calculations of empire: tithes of blood.

In *The Quality of Sprawl: Thoughts about Australia*, Les Murray suggests
that Australian society has sometimes felt overwhelmed by the splendours
of the natural world. Asked by some councillors what their municipality
needed, the poet immediately answered: 'Something wonderful: commis-
sion something wonderful!' This is what all poets are commissioned to
do. Some succeed; some don't. On the evidence of the work reviewed
and mentioned here, there is plenty to admire in the municipality of
poetry in Australia, and more to look forward to.

Special Feature: Vittorio Sereni

Vittorio Sereni (1913-1983) is widely regarded as the finest Italian poet
of the generation after Montale. From *Frontier* (1941), his 'pre-war
book with one foot in the war,' through *Algerian Diary* (1947) which
reflects his POW experience, to *Variable Star* (1981) and the posthumously
collected work, his poetry is a faithful testimony
to the times: the period of fascist dicatatorship, the vicissitudes of life
in Italy through the years of post-war reconstruction,
the economic miracle of the 1960s and beyond.

Thanks to **Peter Robinson** and **Marcus Perryman** for contributing
their translations to this feature, and to **Silvia Sereni** for permission
to publish.

Peter Robinson

VITTORIO SERENI'S ESCAPE FROM CAPTURE

Vittorio Sereni's first real encounter with America occurred between
eleven o'clock and midnight on 24 July 1943 – just two days before his
thirtieth birthday and one before Mussolini's fall from power in Rome.
That April, having narrowly missed becoming air reinforcements for the
North Africa campaign when the runway at Castelvetrano was bombed,
Sereni's Pistoia Division was sent to form part of the defence of Sicily,
preparing for anticipated Allied landings in the west of the island near
Trapani. However, on 10 July the invasion of Sicily began in the east at
Gela and Syracuse. This meant that Sereni and his fellow soldiers were
trapped in a pocket which, during the following two weeks, tightened
around them. When the American 82nd Airborne Division arrived at
Paceco, the Italians surrendered with barely a shot being fired. They were
first imprisoned in the sports stadium at Trapani, then, on 15 August,
shipped across the Mediterranean to near Bizerta. The first plan was to
send these POWs to camps in the USA, and Sereni was aboard ship at
Oran when news of the Italian armistice arrived. On 8 September
General Badoglio's government signed a separate peace with the Allies.
As a result of his changed status (from enemy prisoner-of-war to
captured soldier of a co-belligerent) the poet didn't cross the Atlantic,
but spent one and a half years in various American-run camps in Algeria
near Oran. His final six months of captivity were at the Fedala Camp in
French Morocco on the Atlantic coast near Casablanca.

In two prose pieces from many years later, 'The Capture' and
'Twenty-Six,' Sereni contemplates an alternative fate. The former, first
published in 1963, is a fictionalized account of an incident that may have
happened between his capture and the voyage to Africa. Returning from
a small island where he has acted as interpreter for an American platoon
effecting the surrender of an Italian garrison, Franchi – the Sereni figure
– is sitting on a crate of grenades:

> it would have been enough to glance meaningfully at the soldiers
> captured with him, to make a circle round the crates of grenades the
> enemy had imprudently put aboard as trophies of war. He was himself
> sitting on one of those crates. It wouldn't have been difficult to flip the
> latch, to get up swiftly, lift the lid …

Sereni describes how a glance at George, the American officer, whose
company Franchi enjoys, effectively ends this fantasy of escape: 'Not

because a farcical tenderness had intervened; but the very way of looking at that face had told him that he, personally, was not made for such adventures.' In 'Twenty-Six,' written during 1969, he imagines how the remnants of his trapped regiment might have taken the corporate decision to filter through the Allied lines, to cross the Straits of Messina, and perhaps form one of the first partisan units. Such an alternative fate has support in historical fact. The Allies captured Messina on 17 August after over 62,000 Italian troops (according to Sereni's 'The Sands of Algeria') had been evacuated. The poet imagines how he and his companions would

> slip away through the opposing ranks no longer men in arms but companies of pilgrims – by dry fords, skirting riverbeds, within sight of metropolises which are rubble against the light — scattered, reunited by prearranged routes and rendezvous, filtering, breaking through: pouring out finally, motley and bare, but already rich in other resources, deftnesses and crafts, unanimous in the furrow of one of the possible futures — which is what I was in search of down there …

'Twenty-Six' is both a memoir of his revisiting the sites of his capture, and a meditation on the relationship between those events and a life of writing. It is as if his fate as a man and his destiny as a writer divide and turn upon each other with the events of that night in July 1943. The loss of such freedom as was allowed in fascist Italy for his first thirty years would release his imagination to contemplate possible futures. His art would eventually come to flourish in the division between the endured and the imaginable, in the conflict between what can be conceived and what turns out apparently to be inevitable.

Giacomo Debenedetti has written of how, in Part Four of *Diario d'Algeria*, with the dialogue between the first Allied soldier fallen on the Normandy beaches and the poet in Camp Hospital 127, 'history entered into Sereni's poetry.' However, Giovanni Raboni, introducing a 1998 edition of *Diario d'Algeria* (1947), has sought to qualify this declaration. After all, as he notes, what Sereni says to the dead soldier is not promising as an indication of someone acknowledging the role of history for his art. In the poem's first verse a hand has touched him on the shoulder murmuring 'pray for Europe / as the New Armada / drew on the coast of France':

> But if you truly were
> the first fallen splayed on the Normandy beaches,
> you pray if you can, I am dead
> to war and to peace.

This, the music now:
of the tents that flap against the poles.
It's not the music of angels, it's my own
music only and enough...

The idea of praying 'for Europe' at such a moment could be thought thoroughly ambiguous. The opening of a second front in northern France was to bring a year of fighting and suffering to armed forces and civilians alike. Equally, it could be taken to mean that Europe is about to be saved from the horrors of the fascist regimes, and he should pray that the Allies are successful. Sereni, in the poem, finds himself in no position to commit to either form of prayer. He is metaphorically, while the Allied soldier is actually, 'dead / to war and to peace.' All the poet has is his marginal music, that of the poem. These lines turn the move towards an aesthetic realm in which history can be resisted upon its self. In Sereni's verse the aesthetic does not transcend history; but neither does history bully the poet into opportune pieties.

Sereni's poetry and prose might at first seem to be for the Second World War what Ungaretti's were for the First. The younger poet calls himself 'his son' in a 1970 piece prompted by the older man's death. Yet this affinity conceals innumerable ironies. 'Italia' from *L'allegria* ('But your people are borne / from the same earth / that bears me / Italy') is enough to underline how for Ungaretti war service would unite him with the country from which his parents had emigrated to Egypt in 1878. He had not lived in his native land for any length of time until he was serving with its armed forces. When Mussolini, who had been an interventionist in 1915, used the idea of a national humiliation at the battle of Caporetto as a means to gain power in 1922, Ungaretti's war service made him a convenient symbol for national heroism and culture. Sereni notes in the same piece that 'like a son I lived and suffered his illuminations and furies, his insights and errors: a bit like for Italy, since Ungaretti was, and how, also Italy.'

Yet Sereni, born in 1913, was not able unequivocally to identify with his country and its 1930s neo-imperialism. Among his earliest poems is 'Garden Concert,' first published 1935, in the year the League of Nations introduced sanctions in protest against Mussolini's Abyssinian adventure. Here the young poet projects himself into 'gardens all over Europe' where the heat is being counteracted by jets of water:

On the children at war in the borders
it fans out, makes vortices;
sound suspended in droplets
instantaneous

you mirror yourself in the shadowy green;
red and white torpedoes
beat on the asphalt of Avus,
trains head south-east
through fields of roses.

Avus is a racing circuit in Berlin where the 'torpedoes,' Alfa and Auto
Union cars, are battling it out while, elsewhere, the Orient Express
trundles towards Venice. Sereni's poem signals by means of the tacit
sensitivities available to one living under a dictatorship a passive resistance
– one that the poet would come to accuse himself of in his post-war
writings. So it was Sereni's fate to be on the wrong side during the 1930s
and the war – and to find himself enduring those years, passively once
more, and imagining that he could live them as the author of *L'allegria*
had done. Yet just as Ungaretti was soon in conflict with the régime, so
Sereni's father (a customs officer in Luino) left the fascist party in 1924 in
protest against the murder of Matteoti. Sereni's wartime predicament
points to the difficulties encompassing the virtues of patriotism and
loyalty for those living under oppressive governments. However, if it was
Sereni's human fate to find himself on the wrong side during his first
thirty years, it was his destiny as a writer to witness and then explore that
fate.

Among the many creative strands that began with Sereni's imprison-
ment was his involvement with poetic translation. Introducing a selection
from his work in the field, *Il musicante di Saint-Merry* (1981), the poet
recalls being asked by a fellow prisoner to make an Italian poem from a
literal rendering of Edgar Allan Poe's 'The Conquering Worm.' In the
same piece, he cites a passage by Sergio Solmi to describe how the
inspiration to translate may arise:

> The translation is born, in contact with the foreign text, with the power,
> the irresistibility of the original inspiration. At its birth there presides
> something like a surge of envy, a regret at having missed this irrecoverable
> lyric occasion, at having lost it to a more fortunate confrère in another
> language.

In his versions of Ezra Pound's early poems from 1955 and of William
Carlos Williams from 1957-1961, he addressed himself to the freshness
and openness of American modernist experiment. The latter in particular
helped him evolve the more extended and inclusive style of *Gli strumenti
umani* (1965) and *Stella variabile* (1981). This influence is acknowledged
through echo and citation. 'Penny please! Give me penny please, mister'
from 'The Desert Music' may have prompted a memory of Algerian chil-

dren calling to a train-load of prisoners 'give me bonbon good American please' in 'The African Sickness.' 'Works in Progress' quotes Sereni's translation of the lines 'the beds lying empty, the couches / damp, the chairs unused,' from 'These.'

He also translated all of René Char's Feuillets d'Hypnos during 1958, and a selection of later work appeared as Ritorno sopramonte in 1974. With these renderings, the Italian poet was enabled imaginatively to involve himself in the partisan conflict that his imprisonment in North Africa has rendered impossible. In 'The Sands of Algeria,' Sereni describes how hearing about the resistance movements 'tormented us.' Section 138 of Char's wartime aphorisms has the French poet assisting 'one hundred metres away, at the execution of B.' One of Captain Alexandre's companions, about to be shot by the SS, could have been saved if Char had given the order to open fire:

> I didn't give the signal because this village had to be saved at all costs. What's a village? A village like any other? Perhaps he understood, he himself, at that final moment?

Reading Sereni's version on the facing page to the French original we can sense the translator's exclusion from the occasion, and his imaginative involvement, his assistance in this horrible day. The accuracy and restraint of Sereni's rendering, the inclusion of the translator in the process of remembrance and transformation, converts the 'surge of envy' into a living gratitude. In translating American and French poetry he lives out in imagination his other fate (the one unlived) in support of the side he was truly – at a cultural and human level – always on.

Not least of the ironies associated with his life and work is that Sereni's should have been so caught up, not with serene victory but humiliating defeat. His poetry and imaginative prose never forget that he is assisting the cause of European humanism as its defeated enemy, always at the border of the imagined fate sketched in 'Twenty-Six.' Near that memoir's close he evokes a few lines from C P Cavafy's 'Comes to Rest': 'twenty-six years / your phantom's crossed over / now to remain in these lines.' With their help, Sereni writes, he had 'played out the conflict' in his name and 'established a reciprocity by which we found ourselves over and over again imploring forgiveness of each other for the time that had passed unopposed by us.' Thus, unlike Italy in September 1943, he can never switch to the winning side.

His fate was always to be in the wrong, as he makes clear, recalling the Munich agreement of September 1938, at the close of 'In an Empty House' from May 1967. Yet it was his destiny to witness and then, with an unflinching memory of his own, to express it:

Provided there were a story anyway
– and meanwhile in the papers Munich at first light
ah thank goodness: there'd been an agreement —
provided there were a story, exquisite among the swastikas
one September in the rain.

Today *we are* – and anyway we're bad,
part of the evil you yourself should sun and lawn turn overcast or no.

And it's this fidelity to reconsidered experience, achieved through the wedding of the technical and the spiritual in his evolving style, which gives his work its overwhelming cultural importance. It shows how with sustained effort goodness can be born from error and self-betrayal. What's more, its historical memory prevents the slightest righteousness or triumphalism in the representation of the lyrical protagonist. Thus located, Sereni could produce the astonishing counter-factual possibility that concludes his prose piece 'Port Stanley like Trapani,' written in June 1982, only eight months before his death. He imagines how the opposed British and Argentinian soldiers might 'break out of the circle that divides them and…run towards each other, slap each other on the backs or treat themselves to festive kicks up the bottom, and embrace.' The piece ends poised upon the border of a 'a victory over absurdity by means of the unthinkable.' Yes, thinking the unthinkable: that's how Sereni's art is a sustained and sustaining escape from capture.

Vittorio Sereni

from *Frontiera* (1941)

SOLDIERS IN URBINO

These towers high in the memory
when the ramparts are at peace
and the fog is barely
drawing autumn onto these lands,
onto us
two, wandering soldiers. You say,
– *unhappily* – and choke back
a name if a leaf torn from who knows
where brushes against you,
then you speak of a star
which one day once more
over your path will perhaps appear.

Perhaps only from today
will we feel the hour's surge
curving halfway through our century,
even as the wind rocks the lamps
a portico whispers in shadow
and you start at the rumble
of lorries gnawing the mountain.

TERRACE

Suddenly the evening seizes us.
                    You no longer know
where the lake finishes;
only a murmur
skims over our life
beneath a suspended terrace.

We're all hanging
on a mute event this evening
in that torpedo-boat's searchlight
which scrutinizes us then turning vanishes.

Vittorio Sereni

from *Diario d'Algeria* (1947)

BELGRADE
  – to Giosue Bonfanti

            – ... Donau? –
Nein Donau, Sava – as in a dream
the sentry says and a bridge
drums beneath the lingering convoy.
And I don't know what remote depth
of labour and voices from your parapets
celebrates a peaceful hour in Europe
born with you between two chimeras
 – the Danube! the Sava! –
azure in a morning lost,
to come to pass:
unforeseen dream of memories, as
the sentries dream
from the bridges of the Sava
some figure among the trees at random,
a love romance just caught sight of.

Mestre-Athens troop train, August 1942

Vittorio Sereni

from *Gli strumenti umani* (1965)

IL PIATTO PIANGE

Reduced to so few the early spring gathered them –
some gone not far away, removed
a little, some hills or ridges away beyond sight
or earshot, a ringing bell's distance
depending on the wind across the plains,
others lost forever walled up in some work
within pummelling cities.
            And those left behind here?
Down here, they come down here, below stairs
and for days and nights shut within barred exits
every crack stopped *I'll see you, pass, I'll raise*
clubs diamonds hearts spades sheltered from life or rather,
were magnolia or languishing wistaria to bloom,
from life's repetition...
        and no
no platinum cut of brightness on the waters
no fine weather, spring, and the newly betrothed
on the torrent of seed who knows if companions won't set out
for other sailings other fordings
towards darkest woods, currents blazing, black grapes
at the confines of the formless?

So me like them so them like me
like them like me in flight, with words with music
in the ears, a piercing cock-crow – from what distance –
a burning disorder, of swoons? The solitude?
And then in the flame reborn of itself
to be for some moments, me us, solitude?
And six foot under ground?
          O my brave ones...
the spades fall to jacks the clubs to queens –
and the night's poor face is at the gaps
a swamp's tumescent dark
        is dripping
refuse of every kind. But where there's refuse,
says someone alarmed, there's life –

and a blast of wind between walls and doors
with the desperation which, denying, asserts
(it's no gambling den no bordello this respectable house)
the wind's voice will scatter the cards
and us they throw outside.

Note: '*Il piatto piange*' [the plate is crying] is an idiomatic phrase in poker requesting players who have not yet matched the stake to do so; 'when it's raining outside' ('*come quando fuori piove*') is a mnemonic for the suits of cards in Italian: *cuori, quadri, fiori, picche*. Sereni's poem shares its title with Piero Chiara's first novel that concerns card players in Luino, their native town, during the fascist era.

Vittorio Sereni

from HOLLAND

Amsterdam

Chance led me there between
nine and ten one Sunday morning,
turning at a bridge, one of many, to the right
along a canal half iced over. And not
this is the house, but merely
– seen a thousand times before –
'Anne Frank's house,' on the simple plaque.

Later my companion said:
Anne Frank's shouldn't be, it isn't
a privileged memory. There were many
who were broken simply out of hunger
without the time to write.
She, it's true, did write it.
But at every turn, at every bridge, along every canal
I continued to search for her, no longer finding her,
finding her perpetually.
That's why it's one and unfathomable Amsterdam
in its three or four varying elements
which it blends in many recurring wholes,
its three or four rotten or unripe colours
which its space perpetuates far as it stretches,
spirit that irradiates steadfast and clear
on thousands of other faces, everywhere
seed and bud of Anne Frank.
That's why Amsterdam's vertiginous on its canals.

The Interpreter

'Now they're returning. Florid, rowdy
loaded with currency.
They are good clients, can't be turned away.
Information, as much as they want.
Not a word more. It isn't a question
of grudges or retaliation.
But of unflinching memory.'

Volendam

Water here a hundred years back
– repeated Federico the guide –
today *polder*.
     Life
between *polder* and dyke, there's room here
for procreation only
and defence against death.
That's what the faces reddened by the cold say
outside the Catholic mass
at Volendam, the dirge
of the varying wind between sea-walls.
Love is for later, it's for the children
and it is greater. Take heed.

Vittorio Sereni

EARTHLY PANTOMIME

> ...auprès de margelles dont on a
> soustrait les puits.
>   – René Char

Just listen – he says – to that wonderful *cheep* in the trees
as if from branch to branch the poker game were going on
    outdoors:
you can't tell me life's not stupendous.

Clearly he's trying to win me through my verse.
I'd like to reply with a trifle of the mind
another of my own amongst the many
(people struck with moonlight through the porticoes
and one among them, moving between them:
try this fresh delight).

Sure, – I reply though – stupendous. Want witnesses?
Proofs ad infinitum? Counterproofs?
Here's my bitterness from day to day
my intolerance of one man after another
(but these breezes between the shallows and rapids
between torrents and life's respites these balms...)

It seems to suffice: but therefore (blessing, kindly)
well then, take courage!
                Up twistings of stairs
go he and his courage.
                You speak – I call behind –
like a believer in no matter what faith.
And from branching stairs, his face half gone
in shadow, he serenades me with a quote: *¿le gusta
este jardin que es suyo? Evite...*
I finish the phrase from below *que sus hijos lo distruyan*
mimicking his tone.

As if it weren't already ruined, with our own hands:
and you who are so far ahead on justice's
and value's stairs, tell it to your followers and disciples

to your associates, summon them to these glasses
of delight to these displays of freshness
but in communion all of you and at one time.

What's left is a stain a puddle of light
not convinced of itself a well of work with around it
a dancing ring of prisoners (they say) on parole:
they taste of a flash that will come
and behind it, in a chain, all the colours of life
– and it will be unbearable.

Well he seems to understand what they're insisting
where they're heading what they want and don't want
what they deny what ways out they take
the cars on the evening's roundabout
with those pretending at each turn to go away forever
with those pretending at each turn to arrive
behind a new town to start up from nothing
– and first flares
            rustling leaves
                        the senselessness of summer.

Note: the epigraph ['near the rims from which the wells have been
removed'] cites *Fueillets d'Ipnos* no. 91; *cheep* ('cip') is also the sound made
by poker players to signify 'I pass'; '*¿le gust a ... .destruyan*' [It pleases
you, this garden which is yours? Prevent...your children from destroying
it] appears in this form at the end of Malcolm Lowry's *Under the Volcano*.

Vittorio Sereni

from *Stella variabile* (1981)

from A HOLIDAY PLACE

III

> *'memory you still have desires'*
> *you say you don't understand it – or, if you do, don't love*

The two who go along by the river, white and azure,
what will they be saying? Joined or apart
for years I've seen them pass
dancing in the shimmer and the wind.
Steady above the vertiginous, enraptured with lingering gaze
on close hills and further cliffs,
finger indicating, against the light, cities
which perhaps were and never will be –
'All this,' says the woman, 'I'll give you
if you'll fall down and worship me.'
But the man, unequal to the dream and subjugation,
is quickly dispirited, music stirs them no more.
                    And as if nearly none
of this had ever been, she returns
to what she'd been before:
a shadow of the blood and mind
and towards the harbour
after a while they disappear.

It's the same old theatre, the same old war.
Memory forges desires
then is left alone to bleed
over these multiple mirrors.
            But look –
voices come back from the estuary – from moment
to moment look how colours change: from grey
to green, from green to freshest blue.
Then cherish it – from thing to thing
comes the reply, from mirrored to mirroring –

then cherish the memory
for as much as it's uplifted here, dazzles, and is done:
it's all the possible, it's the sea.

Author's Note: The lines in italics at the head of this part are mine from
a poem left uncompleted a number of years ago. This in its turn recalled
another old poem of mine, 'Gli squali' (in *Gli strumenti umani*); 'All this…
if you'll fall down and worship me' is from the Devil's temptation of Jesus
in St Matthew's *Gospel*, Chapter 4, v.9; 'And as if nearly none…they
disappear': the two quotations are from Boccaccio's tale of Nastigio
degli Onesti in the *Decameron*.

Vittorio Sereni

from *Gli immediati dintorni* (1983)

SELF-PORTRAIT

I am, without doubt, a meteoropath. The more so now that I feel out of
sympathy with three of the four seasons: I would be happy if it were
always summer and that no atmospheric variation could disturb it. Being
out of sympathy with the seasons means being out of sympathy with
existence, starting with yourself. Writing is part of existence, though I do
have a doubt about that. The doubt comes, on the one hand, from the
idea that writing represents a slight gain in vitality, and, on the other,
from a symptom of incompleteness, an inadequate aptitude for living
fully. This too is meteoropathy and also explains why I write at intervals;
long, for me extremely long, periods go by in which nothing gets written,
although my thoughts are perpetually going in that direction. These peri-
ods, I ought to say, are not a matter of abstinence, but of genuine
impotence. This is painful to confess – so much so that occasionally I try
to convince myself that it's really a slow assimilation eventually bringing
things into focus, a silence that has not been imposed but is nonetheless
necessary, deriving from something in my own nature. On one occasion I
was even moved to call it 'creative silence.' So the benevolent are mistaken
when they attribute to me (some, even more generously, say it's my
strength) a kind of perfectionism. The fact is that at my age I still haven't
learnt how to sit down and work at a desk, and I don't think I ever will.
It's a pity, because not only do I tell myself that by now I ought to have
learnt, but because I'm also convinced it would do me some good,
curing me, among other things, of meteoropathy. It would, for example,
compensate for the unease that shrieks in me on certain sunny, windy
winter days, which I sense as a deathly distortion. To sit down at a desk,
or rather, to make experiments, I need a mediator. Then, that way I can
and do enjoy it. The mediation may come from a foreign text I'm
tempted to, or, perhaps, have been asked to translate. Much more rarely
it may be another kind of emissary, something I have written earlier and
forgotten. I don't rewrite it, heaven forbid, just repair it here and there if
need be, applying myself with the benefit of hindsight to the three or
four points I remember being dissatisfied with and which had estranged
me, no other word for it, from my own text. Could it be a commissioned
piece of work? Sometimes, yes, provided it coincides with something I'm
interested in at the time, but this is even rarer, and not evidently connected
to (how shall I put it?) the intermittent activity of writing poems with
which my name is almost exclusively associated.

I don't know whether it's also true, to give another obvious example, of the informal talk I am giving myself up to here. Probably not, if I think about how I've forced myself to the desk to fill up a few sheets of paper for this purpose. When someone asks if I'm working on something I don't know what to reply. Painful and elusive enough, my response is: 'Yes, on and off'; or else, less frequently: 'Yes, I've written some poetry.' Work, in this context, for me, means finished work, definitely completed. Much more nebulous and difficult to pinpoint is work in progress: that's to say, the phases and progression of the work. For this reason I'll always envy philologists, historians, archeologists, restorers, and, a little less, critics, especially reviewers, as well as full-time novelists with their large canvasses.

If the person I'm talking to insists and asks me what 'on and off' means, I get embarrassed and become discomforted, as though being asked faithfully to recount, point by point, something extremely personal and private. Such embarrassment is not always shame or bloody-minded-ness, quite the contrary. Those attitudes are contradicted by the desire to launch myself into a description of how, from the initial sensation, or from an accidental occurrence related to it, the first expressive nucleus was formed. I'd want to describe how it was concentrated perhaps in one of those lines that, as they say, is dictated by the gods. I'd say how it seems destined for, already mentally placed at, the beginning, the end, half way or three-quarters through a poem yet to be written. Nonetheless, from the very first moment, this unwritten poem suggests itself in quite precise terms: its outline, width, length, long or short or middling, or whatever. The desire passes quickly because I am aware that never, never could I convey, however involved and interested my listener may be, the intensity with which the imperceptible phenomenon was lived, was welcomed as a little miracle.

If I am then asked about the origin and general sense, or, worse still, the aim of my favourite themes, I get even more embarrassed. Yet it will never be as grave as the embarrassment of the questioner, who'll certainly be left with the impression of having attempted to sound the depths of emptiness. The fact is I don't have favourite themes; or, if I have them, I'm not conscious of it. For one thing there would be the risk of confusing them with certain spiritual dispositions, in other words, of turning them perpetually into the correspondents of particular states of mind, thus blurring them into psychology. Supposing it's possible to speak in some way of thematics, or themes, this only makes sense to me if related to a specific poem, but even then I'm aware that the poem didn't take shape in order to embody any theme.

Naturally, I am not making of these confidences (what else can they be called?) a rule, for me or still less for anyone else. I'm only seeking, in response to what was asked of me, to account for how I see myself in the face of what I write, or better, have written. My reluctance derives from the discomfort of going about the world with the name 'a writer,' more specifically, 'poet.' This designation – which there's nothing to be ashamed of – disturbs me when I think of the separated corps, the inexorably fenced off zoo that, for many reasons and despite many signs to the contrary (which I consider faulty or specious), the writer's and, in particular, the poet's world has become. To be aware of this and at the same time to have staked too much in the course of a lifetime on the dominating thought of poetry, here is a grave contradiction from which I suffer and which nonetheless I must confess. It doesn't alter the fact that I'd like to see the world of writers and poets – not of writing, or poetry, not the works – dissolve, the bars be removed from the cages of the zoo currently fencing off that separated corps to which, in spite of everything, I belong. Let's suppose it happens. Outside, there's the jungle, no use pretending otherwise. What path will the un-caged creatures follow? Once again some lines by my friend Giorgio Caproni come to mind, ones I often quote with amusement, yet fully conscious of their gravity:

> Don't ask any more.
> For you nothing's left here.
> You're not one of the tribe.
> You're in the wrong forest.

Some years ago, in Milan, an exhibition was held entitled *The Search for Identity*, a title disputed by some as a mere pretext, a gratuitous banner under which to bring together a number of more or less worthy, more or less representative works. True or false, the title nonetheless suggested a provisional justification, a reply to otiose questions like why do you write or, in general, work, and for whom. It responds to a recurrent concern in our time, so inescapable nowadays that every piece of work or show founded upon an expressive wish is said to be nothing but a search for identity. Nowadays, when no one would any longer feel able even to conceive of a definition of art, or poetry, still less to conceive of it once and for all, it's difficult to imagine that a painting or poem or anything undertaken with artistic intentions has any other significance. This would not be a definition of the fact that signs are put on canvas or words on paper, but certainly a motivation or, frankly, an exculpation for works of this kind: expressing, precisely, the search for identity. One's own naturally, and others' or rather others' with respect to one's own, and vice versa. As far as I'm concerned now – and let me emphasize the now – I wouldn't know what other reasons or justifications to give for what I've written or can imagine writing in the future. This search, at least in my case, cannot yield other than sporadic recognitions, that is, partial and transitory identifications – and self-identifications; it is a hunt that doesn't presuppose a final, comprehensive prey. It lives, if it lives, on a contradiction from which filters, on and off, a primary (call it deluded, call it unfulfilled, call it unrequited) love of life.

– 1978

Note: Sereni cites in its entirety Giorgio Caproni's 'Cabaletta dello stregone benevolo' from *Il Muro della terra* (1975).

Marco Sonzogni

A RICH TRADITION

Edited by Jamie McKendrick, *The Faber Book of 20th-Century Italian Poems* (Faber and Faber, 2004), £ 12.99.

One of the books I treasure most is the first edition of George Kay's *The Penguin Book of Italian Verse* (1958). I found it, many years ago, and bought it for a few pounds in a second-hand book sale held annually in Trinity College Dublin. I was surprised it had survived more expert eyes. Albeit dated, that anthology remains a somewhat 'evergreen' point of reference, if not term of comparison for anthologies of poetry in translation. Indeed, it has served Anglophone scholars of Italian poetry and translation studies. More importantly, it has helped generations of readers with little or no Italian to access one of the richest poetic traditions in western literature. As we read in the publisher's blurb for this 'new anthology,' 'Italy has produced some of the most inventive and controversial poetry of the past one hundred years.' In his introduction and preface, the editor – a fine poet in his own right as well as one of the most gifted translators of Italian poetry in English (he is currently completing a translation of the poetry of Valerio Magrelli) – highlights two important aspects, which should be kept in mind when 'assessing' the sense and significance of this or, indeed, any other anthology.

Firstly, McKendrick explains in the introduction, 'what this anthology wants, and wants to be, [...] is both a personal gathering as well as a collection that I hope works sufficiently well in English to give at least an idea of the breath and complexity of Italian poetry in this period.' This is an important 'admission,' for want of a better word: often omitted by editors, it is pertinently prompted by reviewers. The compilation of an anthology rests on a crucial contradiction. It is meant to be (or 'wants to be,' in the editor's words) a 'comprehensive selection' based on objective criteria. Yet it ultimately comes to life as the result of subjective – hence, inevitably, also 'partial,' in every sense of this adjective – choices. More importantly, McKendrick is, *de facto*, mapping the territory of *his* anthology: to illustrate the variety and complexity of twentieth century Italian poetry 'sufficiently well in English.' In other words, this anthology is designed to document the 'development' of Italian poetry over the last one hundred years to an English-speaking readership.

In spite of this clear (to this reviewer, at least) 'declaration of intentions,' several reviewers have quickly criticised the editor and the publisher for the absence of the original texts and of biographical (and explanatory) notes for each poet. In the second paragraph of his recent review of this book for *The Independent*, for example, Paul Bailey has referred to both, considering the latter 'a more serious omission.' These objections, however pertinent, seems to me to lose some, if not all, of their relevance, when 'verified' against the editor's indications.

Secondly, as we read in the short preface, McKendrick points out that 'personal taste, the availability of translations and the perceived standing of the individual poets have all shaped the making of this book.' This threefold 'clarification' is also very important. The reference to personal taste testifies to the editor's awareness that the matrix of any anthology is, as I have already remarked, a combination and a balance of objective and subjective parameters and decisions. McKendrick refers to the availability of translations as a constructive challenge rather than dismissing it as an editorial excuse. Not every poet, and this applies to 'major' and 'minor' ones (I reluctantly rely on this debatable distinction, exploited and exhausted by T S Eliot, for the sake of clarity), has enjoyed the 'coverage' – to use a buzzword of modern media – of translation. Anthologies, therefore, can offer the opportunity to 'rectify' such gaps. This is, unquestionably, one of the merits of McKendrick's anthology. As far as the perceived standing of the individual poets is concerned, it is virtually impossible – and, to a certain extent, pointless – to try and satisfy everybody's poetic palate and critical categories.

In this reviewer's opinion, McKendrick's anthology addresses and overcomes these three 'obstacles' with poetic sensitivity and editorial maturity. In addition, as it were, to the 'usual suspects' – D'Annunzio and Marinetti, Govoni and Gozzano, Saba and Cardarelli, Penna and Pavese, Bertolucci and Sereni, Caproni and Pasolini, Luzi and Levi, Fortini and Zanzotto, Sanguineti and Magrelli; not to mention, as Dante would have called them, *le tre corone*: the 'three crowns' of Ungaretti, Montale and Quasimodo – the reader can 'sample' poets as different as Bassani and Buffoni, Giudici and Gibellini, Ripellino and Raboni; as well as other distinctive yet underrepresented poets such as Nelo Risi, Bartolo Cattafi, Giorgio Orelli, Luciano Erba, Gianni D'Elia. It is a pity, however, that the tormented genius of Alda Merini (arguably the most gifted Italian poet of the twentieth century) and the sensual virtuosity of Patrizia Valduga are not included in the small but significant (and talented) legion of women-poets that includes Maria Luisa Spaziani, Amelia Rosselli, Biancamaria Frabotta, Rossana Ombres, Patrizia Cavalli and Antonella Anedda.

Covering the 'many different schools' of twentieth century Italian poetry – from the nationalisms of D'Annunzio and Marinetti to the *Crepuscolari*; from the cryptic verse of Hermeticism to the 'revolutionary' poetry of Gruppo '63; from the 'novelties' of *I Novissimi* to the political commitment of the *terza generazione* – McKendrick has paid tribute to the inventive and controversial progress of a poetic tradition that, whilst carrying with it the inevitable and intimidating inheritance of its founders, Dante and Petrarch, has moved – and is moving – beyond the deep footprints of its ancestors. He has also successfully documented the historical, cultural and linguistic multiplicity (the complex and delicate issue of poetry in dialect is another story for another day and another anthology) of a nation whose intellectual identity and creativity has always grown out of its often contradictory and painful diversities. In view of all this, the first and last poet in this anthology – Gabriele D'Annunzio, with his pompous persona of *poeta-vate* (even though he is largely neglected in academic circles and curricula, he remains the undisputed begetter of twentieth-century poetry and poetic language), and Valerio Magrelli, with his anti-rhetoric genius of *poeta-accademico* – are, therefore, an appropriate and symbolic choice.

For his selection of Italian poets as well as of translators – himself being one of the most reliable and inspired 'mediators' with Geoffrey Brock, Simon Carnell, Andrew Frisardi, Jonathan Galassi, Eamon Grennan, J G Nichols, Peter Robinson and Harry Thomas – McKendrick has convincingly managed to wear the heavy hats of poet, translator and editor in one. So a couple of spelling slip-ups (Sbarbero and Giudice instead of Sbarbaro and Giudici) in an otherwise impeccably edited volume are quickly forgotten. *The Faber Book of 20th-Century Italian Poems* is a testimony to the editor's profound knowledge of contemporary Italian poetry and sensitivity to the 'exact art of translation,' as George Steiner has defined it. It is also a refreshing reassurance that, like Carcanet, Faber and Faber too is committed to poetry in translation. If Robert Frost maintained that poetry is precisely 'what gets lost in translation,' Seamus Heaney has encouraged us, in theory and in practice, to 'discover what survives translation's true.'

There is plenty of poetic truth to discover in Jamie McKendrick's anthology of twentieth century Italian poetry.

Postscript: If it is difficult to compile a comprehensive anthology, it is impossible to 'represent' it with a couple of poems. For this simple and practical reason, I have chosen – conveniently but also symbolically – a poem by the first poet included in Jamie McKendrick's anthology, Gabriele D'Annunzio, and a poem by the last poet, Valerio Magrelli.

Gabriele D'Annunzio [1863-1936; *b. Pescara, Abruzzi*]

THE SHEPHERDS

September – let's be off. Time to migrate.
Up there in the Abruzzi now my shepherds
are leaving the folds and moving to the sea,
climbing down the savage Adriatic –
which is green like the pastures in the mountains.

They have drunk deeply at the Alpine fountains,
hoping to make a taste of that home water
stay in their exiled hearts to comfort them,
and on the way for miles deceive their thirst.
They've cut themselves new rods of hazelwood.

They drop to the plain by the old droving road,
as if along a silent river of grass,
treading the footprints of their ancestors.
Oh hear the cry of the first to recognise
the shimmering of the sea against the beach!

And now the flock is walking down a reach
of shoreline. Nothing changes in the air.
The sun is fading all that living wool
until it looks the colour of the sand.
Rinsing of water, trampling feet, sweet sounds.

And why am I not there among the shepherds?

– Translated by **Alistair Elliot**

Valerio Magrelli [*b. 1957, Rome*]

THE TIC

Gestures that go astray
appeal to me – the one
who trips up or upturns
a glass of... the one who forgets,
is miles away, the sentry
with the insubordinate eyelid
– my heart goes out
to all of them, all who betray
the unmistakable
whirr and clunk
of the bust contraption.
Things that work are muffled
and mute – their parts just move.
Here instead the gadgetry,
the mesh of cogs, has given up
the ghost – a bit sticks out,
breaks off, declares itself.
Indeed something throbs.

– Translated by **Jamie McKendrick**

Gréagóir Ó Dúill

THE LANGUAGE SHIFT

Irish poetry is written in both the official languages of the country. All the poets who write in Irish, and their readers, have a native or near native competence in English. Some of those who write in English, and some of their readers, have a knowledge of Irish ranging from the negligible to the native. All writers of Irish recognise the strength of the presence of English in Irish life and poetry. Reciprocity is not necessarily always accorded. The major influences on poets – the other writers they read, conversation in the supermarket, media, opportunities to earn one's crust – are so many in English that the maintenance of creative, imaginative and intellectual life in the lesser-used language becomes a daily challenge.

Poets, however, deal in linguistic challenge. It is one source of that frisson of conflict which is essential to art. Poets have always walked along and across the border between languages and may use the border-crossing of translation as a way to deal with a dry period. Liam O'Flaherty's poems and short stories in Irish, his native language, equal his larger work in English; Patrick Pearse worked successfully in both languages; Denis Devlin moved imaginatively from French to Irish to English. This has gone on for some time – in the eighteenth century, Eoghan Rua Ó Súilleabháin attempted to *plámás* his way out of the Navy with a praise-poem in English for Admiral Rodney. More recently, Ó Ríordáin admitted the seductive charm of the larger language enfolding him, while Ó Direáin found himself doggedly setting his teeth to burn the stump as he had burnt the candle, and to continue to develop his art in his native language. Behan wrote a few poems in Irish at about the time Beckett was shifting into French, but the bulk of his work was in English. MacLiammóir's English birth and upbringing does not prevent his poetry in Irish being still enjoyed.

The pre-*Innti* poets in Irish, in the fifties and sixties of the twentieth century, showed the bilingual nature of the situation clearly. Conleth Ellis moved into Irish with sensitivity. Eoghan Ó Tuairisc admitted the then – mid 1960s – advantages, in cash terms, of writing in the smaller language, and was successful in both. Michael Hartnett nailed his colours to the mast, sacrificed a growing reputation in English, and found Irish was not the language to buy pigs in – or much else, for that matter. Pearse Hutchinson has maintained a strong and rich Irish language thread to his work, often paralleling his themes and concerns in English, much as Eithne Strong did. He does so while consistently engaging in translation as did Hartnett, as does Rosenstock. Mícheál Ó Siadhail provided much of his original Gaelic work in an English version, went on to write new work – it seems – in English only.

The *Innti* poets consciously engaged in bilingual activity, gaining and consolidating a large and international audience by facilitating and presenting translations of their work. This was not new, but their youth, freshness and energy created a new dynamic which ensured the continuing presence of Irish at the centre of the poetic culture. Issues of fidelity, even of intellectual copyright, arose. Some translation was so free as to be a form of cultural colonialism and the poets could have a feeling that they had been hijacked. Which was the real work? For its own reasons, the larger poetic culture of English accepted certain Irish language poetic norms more than others – folklore rather than history, rural rather than urban, magic rather than science, eastern rather than western, wonder rather than investigation – and, by rewarding what it preferred, influenced creativity and critical response in the smaller language. English poetic culture released Gaelic poetry from constraints which had not, in fact, been there.

Although Irish shows some signs of having avoided the bowdlerisms of Victorian urban culture, and a strong current of celebration of sexuality, anti-clericalism and political dissent can be traced back through Irish language poetry and songs for hundreds of years, the cultural image of Irish, nevertheless, was to a large degree created in the twentieth century by a conservative state and an even more conservative educational system which did not seek to foster an awareness of elements of intellectual freedom. Some Irish poetry taught even today to mature secondary school students does not compare well with the sweep, complexity and challenge of some of the poetry in English. The degree of conservatism of choice, of the lack of change in the canon, can be unsettling to a developing and active poet.

The border country between the two languages can be inhospitable. Hartnett and Ó Tuairisc, even Ó Ríordáin before them, found the Irish language market ultra-conservative, given to the wagging finger of the conservative language purist, scrupulous as to grammar and syntax and traditional norms. The post-*Innti* practice of face-to-face translation strains the space of editors and may test the generosity of fellow poets in English competing for the same space. The very success of translators and of English language openness to the Gaelic tradition has meant that not everyone accepts as centrally important the maintenance of that tradition in its own medium, so Clarke, Kinsella, Heaney and Montague and others can be presented as ensuring its continuance in a new guise in English.

Other factors can operate. I do not think that my own experience is unique. I now find that, after eight collections, a selected, two anthologies, a collection of short stories, a literary biography and much reviewing, editing and adjudicating in Irish I have started to write in English. I am still sorting out the reasons. One is the erosion of ideology, or the form of ideology which underpinned my daily decision to go on writing in Irish. Maltese has more status, even in the Gaeltacht area in which I spend most of my time. Another reason, more importantly, is a recognition that English is my maternal language. A professional writer must see his or her maternal language as a key resource, and English as a particularly rich one, a resource deserving to be exploited. English is also the maternal language of much of my actual and potential market. Although there is much precedent for writing in a language other than the maternal, and the subject is an international and recognised one, the advantages of using the maternal have become compelling to me.

Then there is the question of translation – if one is fortunate enough to engage the interest of a competent and sympathetic translator, as has happened to me only recently. A dependence on translation entails loss of control. A comparison of the English versions of the most-translated texts in contemporary Irish by Ní Dhomhnaill and Ó Searcaigh reveals, in my view, an excessively wide variation in meaning and style. Some contemporary poets in Irish do not seek translation into English because they think such translation undercuts their individual contribution. I used to think that, but translation can offer much if it results from a co-operative effort, if it creates a common ground, an overlap between fidelity and free-range exploration.

The languages differ. Irish has a stronger aural/oral base partly because it plays the vowel rather than the consonant, enjoys assonance more than English does. Print and mass-literacy came late to the Irish language culture and much poetic dissemination was by memorisation and recitation. The normal English sentence structure is subject – verb – object, while Irish fronts generally with the verb, putting the action rather than the subject or agent in the most influential position. This means that Irish stresses the act, not the actor, that the individual is subsumed in the action, just as the prepositional pronoun suggests that the at-ness is greater than the me-ness in the way we say at me, *agam*. Irish retains dialect differentiation, and the sort of job a good poet does can often entail use of dialect: but this unfortunately does not assist comprehension across an already small readership. English, on the other hand, is probably richer in nuances of register – Irish calls a spade a spade. The poet and the reader in Irish may have problems with reference, although the intimacy of the market may overcome these. In English the very scale of the culture can blunt reference. Irish has a tendency to refer to place, assuming a static rural society, and to the body, while what is easily expressed in English may more likely be motion, thought, abstraction. The languages have somewhat different senses of time, for example with Shakespeare's seven ages of man based on the decade, the Irish *fiche bliain ag fás* based on the score. The imprecisions and wide-ranging definitions in that handbook of poets, Dinneen's Dictionary, are famous; English dictionary definitions are likely to be more precise. What Frank O'Connor called *The Backward Look*, the Gaelic tendency to look for the future in the past, and value the lack of change, can be matched with a tendency to look for heroes rather than groups and cultures. The scale of English culture puts a premium on change and challenge, on opportunity and event.

The Irish language writer lacks life models. Very few prose writers and almost no poets can base their work on a close knowledge of an Irish-speaking community. The linguistic usage of Belfast, the playground language of the Gaelscoil, the speech-practice of younger people in the Gaeltacht, these are unsatisfactory models for many forms of poetry unless used with a fantastic creative licence. Precision and realism are almost unattainable and the work of even Gaeltacht writers – Ó Conghaile in fiction, Ó Searcaigh in poetry – often shows a flight from reality. We see the same tendency in the work of non-native or near-native speakers such as Titley and Ní Dhomhnaill.

But there are other reasons why I am concentrating more on writing poetry in English. My 50th birthday was followed not long after by the start of the new millennium – a time to concentrate the mind on the future. I have also, since then, been engaged in the Poets' House, Falcarragh, Co Donegal, teaching MA students in creative writing, poetry. The work is very largely through English – we have recently had one candidate for the degree who offered Irish work, and her, Mary Reid's, collection has just been published by Coiscéim. Most of the students choose the English language option. I teach the intricacies of an Irish poetry course in both languages, Yeats to Meehan and Jenkinson. The students are all committed apprentice poets. Teaching the poetry of the twentieth century to them, concentrating on the nuts and bolts as these are not apprentice critics but poets, means I have been infected with, galvanised by the way English works. Then to go on to the weekly workshop and see their own poetry take shape, facilitate their redrafting, their growth, has engaged me in a creative effort based on the English language. So, I have swung my efforts across the linguistic border.

Another change. It is over a dozen years since I bought a house in the Donegal Gaeltacht, to spend most of my time there. This had the result of changing the linguistic intensity, the themes and the colour of my verse. Now it seems that much of my work may be in English. Lagan

Press have accepted the first English language collection. I have started another. But all of this has brought the realisation (which underpinned my move to the Gaeltacht in the first place) that the writing of poetry is a social act. Máire Mhac an tSaoi has referred to the appalling isolation of those working in Irish. Recently I have spent a semester teaching contemporary literature and creative writing at postgraduate and under-graduate level in Queen's University, Belfast. Through Irish. While nothing changes utterly, and no terrible beauties are born, I may sense interior movement which I do not understand. A sort of perne in a gyre.

THE LANGUAGE SHIFT

Migrating now, on my own, tentative but definitively
day by day, line by line
into the worked landscape of a different language,
I sometimes see
thousand-year-old attitudes expressed unspoken
in, say, the logical progression of subject – verb – object,
agent – action – result, stress on individual responsibility,
on bobbin and bible,
while we said verb – subject – object
as though the agent was less, subordinate to the act,
just any one of a million peasants, of a thousand prison guards.

Thus, again, the verb 'take off' means
the mutual removal of spectacles, the blind foolishness of a kiss,
means imitation as the sincerest form of mockery,
means planes shrugging loose for another continent.
Not in the language I have left, where the sense
is more to reap, and not to sow, to decapitate.

How to retain them both, then, as I move, the slant sense
of perspective, the dance of railway tracks, steel smiling in the sun?
How to ensure the dust stays on my sandals as I walk?

James J McAuley

THREE DUBLINERS

Paul Perry, *The Drowning of the Saints* (Salmon Publishing, 2003), €12.
Enda Wyley, *Poems for Breakfast* (Dedalus, 2004), €10.
Philip McDonagh, *Carraroe in Saxony* (Dedalus, 2003), €10.

What have we here? One female and two male poets; two first collections, the other with her third book; two stalwart Ireland-based poetry publishers; and all three poets are well-travelled Dubliners (though one may be from Carraroe, since the bio-note doesn't state his birthplace). Well, there's a lot of fuss made these days about statistics, so we ought to throw them out there. Then the people who refer to the arts as a 'sector' can nibble a few chicken-wings while they (a) contemplate a way of getting much better world-wide distribution of Irish publications (unlikely: we might break free-market 'sector' rules); and (b) congratulate themselves that two of these poets have been able to avail of the residencies and bursaries funded by the Arts Council. But enough of this carping.

Poets nowadays have a very wide range of techniques to avail of, though one very rarely now finds a poet working exclusively in strict metrical verse. However, most who use open forms are likely to include a sonnet or villanelle or two, or at least a loosely rhymed, loosely metred – what? – *ballade imaginaire*? – to show they're keeping in touch with – what? – the Tradition? Or a Poetry Workshop group? Even so, those of us who caught the poetry habit around the middle of the last century, mainly by reading a lot of the seriously addictive stuff from the previous twenty-five or so, have had to adjust our perspectives more than somewhat in the past half-century. A deceptively radical shift has gradually moved us from measuring a poem's worth by (a) the author's insight into the subject and its relation to 'how we live now,' and (b) his/her success in uniting form with content – to (a) understanding how well the poet deploys language to connect his/her images to (b) an inner psychic stream of imagery, from which the poem receives authentic form. (I'm afraid I've never fully grasped deconstruction, although like *Le Bourgeois Gentilhomme* I may be actually practising it without knowing, like a primitive churl, pawing through troves, looking for jewellery, useful weapons, warm cast-offs…)

These collections present distinctively lively cases in point. None of the three consists entirely of metrical verse (often erroneously referred to as 'formal'); nor entirely of 'open' or 'free' forms (never referred to as 'informal'). Enda Wyley and Paul Perry use nonce forms, i.e. derived from subject and/or tone. But throughout their work are persistent reverberations from the oldest English traditions: Anglo-Saxon strong-stress anvil-strokes; the oar-stroke quatrains of the Border Ballads (with their Gaelic underpinnings); the couplets and tercets of the Cavaliers and Metaphysicals. Philip McDonagh, on the other hand, makes no bones about his ties to Classical and Continental traditions – and a few more quite exotic sources.

As to other aspects, especially choice of subjects and approaches to same, you'd imagine the three of them were adamantly striving to keep as far from each other as possible – allowing, of course, for the pitiful fact that we're all writing about what Dylan Thomas (or Bob Dylan?) called 'Mirth, Compilation, and Debt.' While they're all writing about writing (*pace* W Stevens), Enda Wyley's voice is quiet, one-to-another, gentle, amused; Paul Perry's has something of the eager declamatory enthusiasm of Whitman hearing America singing, or singing the body electric; while Philip McDonagh writes elegant, reflective verses with the powerful undertones of one who has seen and heard much, and chooses carefully what must be uttered.

Paul Perry arrives garlanded with a degree from Brown University, writing fellowships from Miami and Houston, residencies in Longford and the University of Ulster (current), and an enviable array of prizes and publications (including *PIR*, of course). Regardless of all this loot, his poetry is brimful of imaginative energy and tumbling surreal rhetoric, insolently crashing through every Poetry Workshop barrier any 'leader' could throw up ahead of him. Many are poems of place, but widely various in time and location, from early Dublin childhood to Chetumal, Mexico/Belize, to Sweden's Gotland Island; from New York to Chicago to Paris and back to mythic 'Mulcahy's Farm' and 'The Red Dogs of Wicklow,' to 'The Bats at Annaghmakerrig' and 'Slowly Home' to Dublin.

His singularity is rooted in how he's passionate and playful at the same time, and how he takes liberties with continuity and logic and still keep us in touch with his drift. He's wordy – downright garrulous at times – but, hell, let's just go with the flow. 'Tonight, the sea' is characteristic, though perhaps somewhat muted:

> Tonight, the sea calls out
> and you are here circling Cnoc na Crocaire,
> poor witness watching
> the shadows ride the dark tracks of night
> and the rain shoot down
> into a scaffold of grief,
> listening to the lament of the waves
> working the past into a frenzy of surf,

> envisioning the fear the mariners felt.
> But really, what can you do? Stand,
> shiver on the shore and ruminate?
> Is there anything to salvage from this sea?
> This is all a gesture of longing.

Workshop pundits would have the poet reduce that passage to a slick, distanced presentation of the scene, and none of that arguing. And I would certainly argue that the rhetorical centre of a few poems – 'Looking for beauty in a crab-pool' for example – can be unconvincing and heavy-handed for one who moves his readers along so briskly. All found, this is a most enjoyable collection, and I've no doubt a few re-readings will discover further layers of satisfaction.

Enda Wyley's third Dedalus collection advances her stature considerably. Not that her earlier work was below par in any significant way; but there's now an assured reliance on her strengths – economy of structure and clarity in description – and a broader sweep of the 'inner eye' over her chosen subjects, from love-poems to political satire. Not every poet would chance a subject like 'Cutting Hair on New Year's Day,' moving the bemused reader from a gull's-eye view of a sunken bike in the Liffey, along Ormond Quay, back (in time and place) up to Father 'Flash' Kavanagh's fast Mass in St Audeon's, and back to –

> the congregation below in Adam and Eve's
> staring up the old hill in envy,
> freezing from praying too long.

– before the fourth stanza depicts the New Year's Day haircut and its cool aftermath, dealing with the metaphysical undercurrent without foregoing its rueful humour.

'At Work' rings the changes on this theme, with its listing of commonplace domestic objects and then the more-or-less usual sources (and resources) of domestic stress (and bliss), and its almost querulous resolution:

> We meet bleary-eyed, silent –
> Each knowing the other well.

These new poems attest to a seasoned restraint, an avoidance of flourish or overstatement. Thus, she can rely on her astute arrangement of the imagery she has so carefully selected.

Carraroe in Saxony is, for all intents and purposes, Philip McDonagh's début. (Some poems were included in *Dedalus Introductions* in 1989). Like

Denis Devlin – in more ways than this – he now joins a small, distinguished group of poets who have represented the nation as diplomats. While posted in London, 1994-99, he was involved with developing the Peace Process; he has just recently been appointed our Ambassador to the Holy See.

The governing tonality of this collection is restrained, distanced: the 'voice' has composed itself judiciously before utterance, and yet the undercurrents of affection, ironic frustration, and constant grief are unmistakable. There are intimacies: lovers are addressed, lost love mourned. The title poem is a masterly eight-page composition, addressed to his late 'Ma,' a beautifully measured elegy for her and for Dresden:

> The slow Elbe swaying with heavy hips
> askance of the Dimítroff bridge
> is overlooked by the dark stone
> of Semper's Opera: soft lights
> for them too, now that they've become
> an item – distant stars that pulse
> unendingly. I jettison
> what would dispel, dilapidate,
> *a moment of no consequence.*
>
> [...]
>
> A wild rose in the ruined church;
> The concave silence that degrades
> our suffering and over which
> our hours are strung lyre-like; the child
> comforted in the dark – for us,
> Ma, are the Connemara rain,
> our element; a time like this
> the right time for a taking leave.

The classic Graeco-Roman mask of tragic irony is worn throughout this and several other poems, in deftly turned lines of metrical but wonderfully varied verse. 'In Fluntern Cemetery' is an elegant English sonnet worthy of James Joyce – and Thomas Grey himself; 'Bewley's of Grafton Street' would bring a wry smile to Louis MacNeice's lips; Catullus is the *genius loci* of much more than the two poems which acknowledge his proximity. I'm astounded that this important work – in print since 2003 – hasn't received the kind of attention it richly deserves. Like Neruda, that other shy diplomat, it's time for Philip McDonagh, already in his fifties, to be acclaimed. You heard it here first at *PIR*, where else?

David Wheatley

BODY SNATCHERS STRIKE BACK

Edited by Don Paterson and Charles Simic, *The New British Poetry*
(Graywolf Press, St Paul, Minnesota), $16.

There comes a point in the life of any poetry reader when he or she faces
what might be called the 'next album test.' It goes something like this.
Consider those poets whose work you admire. You've bought their books
down the years, gone to hear them read, queued for their signatures, but
how much are you really looking forward to their next book? As much as
you are to the next Coen brothers film or the next White Stripes album?
Be honest. How many contemporary slim volumes would you hold onto
over your favourite CDs? Double figures? Fingers of one hand? Not too
many, I hope, the one saving grace of real contemporary poetry being
how precious little of it there is. Anthologies are even worse than the
'next album test.' They're like that scene in *Men in Black* when Tommy
Lee Jones complains about his new mini-disc technology, since now he'll
have to buy the 'White' album again. We already *have* all this stuff, damn
it, so what's the point of duplicate copies?

It's unfortunate the way anthologies get reviewed for their intro-
ductions rather than their contents, but since the contents of this US-
published book will be familiar to anyone over here remotely interested
in the subject (I counted one writer, John Glenday, whose work was new
to me), that leaves us Don Paterson's introduction to talk about. It's a
bizarre performance, confirming all the stereotypical faults of British
poetry and adding some extra just for you. Faults such as: slavish deference
to an imagined common reader, neurotic fear of innovation or anything
too difficult, and a wounded, wary defensiveness in the face of any
criticism. For reasons I fail to grasp Paterson devotes much of the intro-
duction to a group of poets not in his book and whom he doesn't even
bother naming. These are the evil Postmoderns, as against the Mainstream
poets he has included, and yes, he does call them that. Is there a grimmer,
more dismal label to pin on a writer than 'mainstream'? I'd take a knee in
the groin over a pat on the head for being any such thing, any day, but
Paterson has his reasons. These are writers, he wants to reassure us, that
steer a middle course between sestinas-R-us New Formalism and splatter-
gun L=A=N=G=U=A=G=E poetry. These mainstreamers are all-round
regular kinda guys, and unlike their deviant counterparts still use language
to communicate. They're the (not so) young generation and they've got
something to say, unlike those postmodern dingbats holding forth to

their 'academic' audience. Which is presumably why back in the real world roughly half Paterson's mainstreamers have taught creative writing in universities.

Paterson's double-think on this subject is very repetitive, be warned. His pantomime villains are held up as laughable yet ubiquitously evil, insignificant yet powerful enough to have ruined playtime for all the other kiddies. The rightness of the mainstream cause is unassailable, yet must be thumpingly reiterated in the spirit of Hopkins' 'man bouncing up from the table' (Robert Browning, in fact) 'with his mouth full of bread and cheese and saying that he meant to stand no blasted nonsense.' The literary history behind all this couldn't be more conformist or unoriginal. Since the days of high modernism we've learned to live with T S Eliot, just about, but don't go trying any Pound on us. The 1940s too tried to lead us astray, but then along came the 1950s and everything turned out just fine. Our current poetic Happy Meal comes with a heady swill of PR cant: Michael Donaghy's poems are 'perhaps' (exquisite scruple) 'built to last in a way few other poets in the language can currently rival'; Andrew Motion has 'confounded the doubters by emerging as the most energetic and forceful advocate for the art [the laureateship] has seen'; John Burnside's 'radiant meditations have been perhaps' (again!) 'the most quietly and pervasively influential voice to have emerged in British poetry in the last twenty years'; and Jo Shapcott is 'one of the most original voices in the language.'

There is talk of mainstream poets being brave enough to risk sounding mundane: '*original* expression... always runs the risk of cliché; the clear articulation of deep emotion always runs the risk of sentimentality; and taking the chance of being largely understood always runs the risk of being found to be talking a pile of garbage.' Paterson is evidently happy to lead by example. And so on. To confront Paterson's big question, though, every critic should have a line on the mainstream versus *avant garde* debate, and mine is this. There certainly is such a thing as a soft mainstream orthodoxy that deserves nothing but scorn, but at the same time it is very difficult for writers to self-identify as innovative or *avant garde* without falling headlong into sanctimony of the worst kind. For that reason alone it's probably best to avoid such terms altogether where self-labelling is concerned. If there's one thing I despair of, though, in debates about the mainstream and the *avant garde* it's the idea that all innovative writers write to a theory (dangerous, abstract, foreign) whereas traditionalists emote with the untutored genius of those feral children in Sir Thomas Browne who spoke perfect Hebrew. I can think of plenty of *avant garde* critics who write to a system, but poets? It's just a canard designed to stifle debate, and one which Paterson is all too happy to rehash: 'far too few of them... have anything resembling what the

Mainstream would recognise as a real compositional procedure... No: they have systems.' Does Roy Fisher write to a system? Does Thomas Kinsella? Of course they don't. But who knows, maybe Paterson doesn't like them either.

But enough about this stupid tirade, and some more observations on the actual contents. There are thirty-six poets in the book. Time has run out on the Britishness of poets from Northern Ireland, they will be variously pleased or outraged to learn: it's mainland mainstreamers only. Most poets get between four and six pages; John Ash gets eight, but Peter Reading looks orphaned and lost in his paltry three. Poems here that look like turning into anthology fixtures include Paterson's 'Imperial,' Robin Robertson's 'Artichoke' and Ian Duhig's 'The Lammas Hireling,' while others (Shapcott's 'Phrase Book,' Duffy's 'Prayer,' James Fenton's 'Wind') are already so familiar as to be at risk of losing all impact. And is Fenton really a 'New' British poet, even to an American reader? Surely not.

I've berated Paterson for wasting time on writers he omits, but realize I haven't said much myself about the poets who do make it into his book. My only defence is that the resistance I feel to the Paterson 'mainstream' tradition is just too strong: despite my liking for quite a few of these writers (Ash, Didsbury, Greenlaw, Hofmann, McKendrick, Oswald, Reading) I can't accept reading them under the terms this book dictates. So let me at least offer some practical suggestions, as a resident alien in Britain, on how mainstream verse culture in this country might tackle its malaise. First, someone should abolish all poetry competitions, and with them the safe and predictable poems they spawn. Second, some other friendly axe-wielder should write off the deeply philistine National Poetry Day and all its works. Third, publishers should scrap the corrupt practice of solicited pre-publication blurbs, and the shot in the arm they provide to debutant writers who don't deserve to be in print anyway. Fourth, journalists should stop equating contemporary poetry with the same small gallimaufry of regulars on the residency/competition-winning/Radio 4 circuit, and ask someone different for a change. And lastly, someone should reverse the respective standing and reputations of Philip Larkin and J H Prynne, Simon Armitage and the sound poet Jaap Blonk, whose collection of grunts and barks so enlivened the CD that came with the summer 2004 issue of *Poetry Review*. I've no real reason for this last suggestion, apart from how much fun the ensuing confusion would be. And all this without mentioning the Next Generation Promotion, that poetic *Invasion of the Body Snatchers* meets *The Empire Strikes Back*, launched to the sound of a Paterson-soundalike whine in *The Guardian* from Armitage about serving the common reader. Avoid at all costs.

'If a gasometer, for instance, affects his emotions, or if the Marxian dialectic, let us say, interests his mind, then let them come into his poetry,' Louis MacNeice told F R Higgins. Was there a subclause I missed prohibiting this ideal poet from being a postmodernist? I've always thought of postmodernism as a stupid idea, but no more so than 'seamless evolution,' 'consensual meaning,' whatever that means, or the other Leavisite zombies creaking through Paterson's prose. If Carol Ann Duffy suddenly decided to turn postmodernist, that'd be fine by me (there are even some people who think she already is...) 'Don't start from the good old things but the bad new ones,' as Bertolt Brecht told Walter Benjamin. Be a 'mainstream' poet even, if that's what turns you on. Be whatever you want, but come up with better reasons for it than the mix of self-righteousness and self-pity that underpins this book.

Paterson concedes the existence of 'a handful of attractive voices' among the postmoderns, but nevertheless hasn't included them here. Why not, if they're as good as he says they are? Because from the position argued in his introduction the existence of alternative styles is simply unthinkable. The mainstream is all there is, and all there shall be, promos, prizes and anthologies like this without end, Amen. And that's a terrible thought.

Gerald Dawe

HAUNTING LANDSCAPES

W S Graham, *New Collected Poems* (Faber and Faber, 2004), £25 hb.
Dorothy Molloy, *Hare Soup* (Faber and Faber, 2004), £8.99.

In 'Johnson in the Highlands,' a fine poem from the early 1960s, Iain
Crichton Smith describes the great English writer in the context of his
journey to Scotland in 1773:

> A classical sanity considers Skye.
> A huge hard light falls across shifting hills.
> This mind, contemptuous of miracles
>
> And beggarly sentiment, illuminates
> A healthy moderation. But I hear
> Like a native dog notes beyond his range...

What those 'notes' may be is of course modulated through history, the
tri-lingual tensions, cultural legacies and social dispossession of Scotland
itself. Crichton Smith as a 'native' speaker whose island-mind was shocked
by the fragmentation of contemporary urban life, drew an outraged
inspiration from the damaged, scattered lives of the Scottish Diaspora
and the broken bonds of community that he identified as the outreach of
Thatcher's Britain. His slightly older contemporary, W S Graham
(Crichton Smith was born in 1928, Graham in 1918), after a brief spell of
living and working as an adult in Scotland, left the country for good
(unlike Crichton Smith who remained there until his death in 1998) and
spent the majority of his writing life in Cornwall, where he died in 1986.

If Crichton Smith established a significant national reputation during
his life, Graham, fighting shy of 'national' categories, has been known
very much as a poet's poet. As we all know, these frames of reference are
unfixed as critical fashion changes. Graham, lauded by his publisher, T S
Eliot at Faber, has a revealing publishing record to set alongside the
increasing lack of attention span of the current literary environment.

Four books are published in the 1940s, followed in 1955 by *The
Nightfishing, Malcolm Mooney's Land* in 1970, *Implements in their Places* in
1977 and *Collected Poems* in 1979. Along with all these books, two post-
humous collections and some previously uncollected poems, this *New
Collected Poems*, edited by Matthew Francis, is the perfect companion to
the magnificent work of Michael and Margaret Snow and their edition of
Graham's letters, *The Nightfisherman* (Carcanet, 1999).

New Collected Poems is quite simply one of the books that anyone interested in modern poetry in English should own. At 380 pages the collection places Graham where he rightly belongs in the central park of modernism, a voice that moves from an intoxified belief *in* language towards an almost Beckettian scrutiny of just how good language is, after all is said and done. While the elegiac tenderness that is released in Graham's later volumes, as he laments the passing of friends and fellow artists, may not reach the human scope of Yeats's hymns to love and friendship, they do take us into an emotional force field few other poets can handle without predictability or easy sentiment getting in the way.

Graham's love poems to Nessie Dunsmuir, his partner and wife, stand comparison with William Carlos Williams's *Asphodel* love poetry. It is the suspicion of resolution and chastening self-consciousness of Graham that has troubled critics and put an X against his name: present but not quite correct. Yet to read aloud, for instance, 'The Nightfishing' or 'The Dark Dialogues' (two poems crying out for radio treatment) is to hear what Graham is all about – as storyteller, maker of anecdote, who drifts from timeless time and place to specific here and now, bringing into focus the way we say things and what we think we mean.

Graham's landscapes are as haunting as King Lear's and as breath-taking as Homer's. He knows what he is about as a poet, the ambitions honed to a speaking voice, sometimes in whispers, sometimes lost in the night or outcast in nightmare. Graham, for all the clarity of his language – the vernacular is worked through the syntax and not the other way around – takes us into the mystery of that desperate word, 'communication.'

'A poet doesn't write what he knows,' Graham remarked in a letter to Edwin Morgan, 'but what he doesn't know.' Hard work, in other words, takes the reader into an uninhabited space and discovers things there, feelings, ideas, whatever – as in 'To My Wife at Midnight':

> Are you to say goodnight
> And kiss me and fasten
> My drowsy armour tight?
>
> My dear camp-follower,
> Hap the blanket round me
> And tuck in a flower.
>
> Maybe from my sleep
> In the stoure at Culloden
> I'll see you here asleep
>
> In your lonely place.

How sad that Dorothy Molloy did not survive the illness which struck her down on the eve of the publication of her first collection, *Hare Soup*. It is an accomplished and engaging debut. Born in 1942 and originally from Ballina, Co Mayo, Molloy's densely packed, passionate and coherent volume is an eye-opener. These short lyrics contain rich and impressive evidence of a real poet's gathering experience (sensual, emotional, visual) into imaginatively exciting form. So it is pitiless (and, alas, pointless) to consider what might have come along after *Hare Soup*. The Muldoonesque twists and turns ('Lilies sprouted / in the grass: Amanthus, Agapanthus, / Amaryllis') and telegraphese would probably have morphed into greater self-belief and fluency. Unerringly though Molloy made poems to last, as dramatic in their own way as Robert Browning's monologues and as unique.

There is a physical dimension to her writing which is, if not rare in Irish poetry, at least uncommon. Molloy is unafraid of revealing a passionate life in the lives of her female personae and in the swing between love and joy, and the absence of these things, her poems revel in a kind of tantalizing play. Dresses, colours, names, romances and Romance, food, seascapes, love-scenes cascade throughout this collection even as the darker shadows loom. But the tone is always pitched just so as in the conclusion to 'Fool's Gold':

> I kept your promise in a pyx,
> a bubble on a swizzle stick,
> long after you had gone.
>
> I keep it in a shoebox now,
> fool's gold, protected from the light,
> along with First Communion snaps
>
> and rosaries with pearly beads,
> and baby teeth the fairy-folk
> forgot.

Hare Soup is a fascinating first collection of real achievement and alluring promise, and so it will remain.

Mary O'Donnell

SUMMER HAS FALLEN ASLEEP

Miklós Radnóti, *Forced March: Selected Poems*, translated from the Hungarian by George Gömöri and Clive Wilmer (Enitharmon Press in association with The European Jewish Publication Society, 2003), £8.95.

In Europe, to be born anytime within the first forty years of the twentieth century meant to be imbued with a consciousness of war and the shift from traditional imperial values to newer systems. The concept of 'freedom' held a certain superficial prominence and cachet from Northern Europe right down to the Iberian Peninsula, but in fact poorly masked its opposite: oppression, inequality, racism, genocide. The Empires had crumbled one by one since the assassination of Archduke Franz-Ferdinand in Sarajevo that precipitated World War I, and vast segments of the European political map were to undergo the kind of massive heave that would create new, unimaginable monsters.

It was into such a landscape that the Hungarian poet Miklós Radnóti was born in 1909. His mother died giving birth to him, and this, combined with a poetic vision that was later on to become fundamentally Judeo-Christian in definition, provides one of the vibrato 'notes' throughout his work. Of Jewish origin, he seems to have felt no special attachment to his race or religion. He matured during the *entre-deux-guerres* period and observed the ultra-conservative Hungarian nationalist Admiral Horthy ultimately throw the country into the arms of Hitler. Radnóti, who had graduated from Szeged University with a distinction in Hungarian and French, had an immediate response to the rise of Hitler. From 1934 on, he saw himself as a doomed man, and was quick to respond to the effects of Fascism elsewhere. Everything, it seemed, was closing in on him, and on Hungary. His sense of personal fate was always connected with his empathy for those suffering in the Spanish Civil War.

The translators faced particular challenges in relation to how best to capture the 'message' and rhythms of Radnóti's voice, especially in the Eclogues. The Latin hexameter, for example, has a clear equivalent in Hungarian verse. Translator Clive Wilmer's task was to find an English measure as flexible as the pentameter, yet long enough to provide the dense feeling and integrity of the Virgilian line. In the end he chose an English line of six accents. In the rhymed verse, Radnóti mostly used the syllabic clusters of a native Hungarian system. The translators eventually made different decisions depending on the poem. Although the title-poem, 'Forced March,' is written in a regular form based on Walther von der Vogelweide's *'Owê war sint verswunden – alliu mîniu jâr,'* the translators opted not to reproduce this form, but to adopt their own version of the hexameter. Gömöri and Wilmer provide such information and much, much more in the introduction to a haunting selection from the mature work of a major figure in modern Hungarian poetry.

On a personal level, Rodnóti was content. In 1935 he married Fanni Gyarmati, and this relationship sustained him through the suffering of the years to come. But the doom-ridden landscape of his imagination was to find its place in reality. From 1940 on, he was conscripted into forced labour battalions. Once the Nazis captured Budapest, he was sent to the copper-mines at Bor in Serbia. In 1944, when the prison-camp at Bor was evacuated as the Germans retreated from the Eastern Front, he and his fellow-prisoners began the forced march that was to lead to his death.

As the poems demonstrate, Radnóti was a poet who bore witness to the world around him, whose intensity and art burns within the moral desecration in which he lived. His own response was a profoundly moral one. This is the really arresting thing about the work: he inhabits a world in which the notion of 'moral forces,' 'immoral forces,' and 'morality' itself are part of the currency, are not relative matters that depend on this or that random and meaningless action. Everything has meaning within his perspective. Every moment of beauty enters the foundry of his vision and emerges no less beautiful, but tempered with a fierce sense of doom, as in 'Garden on Istenhegy,' written in July 1936:

> Summer has fallen asleep, it drones, and a grey veil
> Is drawn across the bright face of the day;
> A shadow vaults a bush, so my dog growls,
> His hackles bristling, then he runs away.
>
> Shedding its petals one by one, a late flower stands
> Naked and half-alive. I hear the sound
> Of a withered apricot-bough crack overhead
> To sink of its own weight slowly to the ground.
>
> [...]
>
> And as for you, young man, what mode of death awaits you?
> Will a shot hum like a beetle toward your heart,
> Or a loud bomb rend the earth so that your body
> Falls limb from limb, your young flesh torn apart?

Rodnóti gives voice to a trans-European view of the turmoil of his era in his 'First Eclogue' (1938). This shows a shepherd and a poet discussing the death of Lorca, and the poet's dismay that his murder was scarcely noticed throughout Europe. The poem closes with the poet's insistence on keeping faith with the act of writing and living 'in this frenzied world':

> God bless you. Time I get home, old night will have fallen upon me.
> The butterfly dusk is fluttering, its songs shedding silver sift.

The attention to aesthetics is marked. Rodnóti's morality, combined with his poetic instincts, means that there is neither holding back nor over-ornamentation. Each word is true to the intention of what he feels or observes. While 'The moon bobs on the sky's foam,' he nonetheless wonders at being alive to see it. The forest bleeds, air weighs heavily on the earth, the branches of a tree reach down as if to grasp his throat. Still, the impassioned voice emerges in love poems and poems of endurance. He writes touchingly of the peace of ancient prisons, (in comparison, one presumes, to the grotesque, hate-impelled versions he was now aware of):

> Oh peace of ancient prisons, beautiful
>   Outmoded suffering, the heroic stance
> Sublimely struck, the poet's death, and all
>   Such measured speech as finds an audience –
> How far away they are...
>
> – 'Oh Ancient Prisons'

By the time Radnóti was on the march from Bor, heading westward for Hungary, there can have been little time for writing. Miraculously, he managed to produce 'Postcards,' brief snatches of poems written on the move, despite starvation and weariness, all leading to these final lines:

> I fell beside him. His body – which was taut
> As a cord is, when it snaps – spun as I fell.
> Shot in the neck. 'This is how you will end,'
> I whispered to myself. 'Keep lying still.
> Now, patience is flowering into death.'
> '*Der springt noch auf,*' said someone over me.
> Blood on my ears was drying, caked with earth.
>
> *Szentkirályszabadja*
> *31 October, 1944*

George Gömöri and Clive Wilmer are to be congratulated for bringing this miraculous selection of poems to English language readers.

Pickings and Choosings

DENNIS O'DRISCOLL SELECTS RECENT PRONOUNCEMENTS ON POETS AND POETRY

'Writing a poem is a kind of hunt for language.'
– Jackie Kay, *BBC Radio 4*, March 2004

'Every distinctive poet notices something new about the language.'
– Adam Phillips, *London Review of Books*, 4 March 2004

'Usually, poems come out of a word or a phrase which magnetically pulls other words and phrases round about it – rather than simply coming out of an idea.'
– Robert Crawford, *BBC Radio 4*, March 2004

'One of the great things about being a writer is the extent to which it allows us to invent ourselves. It's like being in a witness-protection program.'
– Paul Muldoon, *The Paris Review*, Spring 2004

'Poetry fills a human appetite: it matters the way cuisine matters beyond nutrition, or lovemaking matters beyond procreation. Like music and dance, it is at the center of human intelligence.'
– Robert Pinsky, *Newsweek*, 12 April 2004

'Poetry is about the spoken word, not about the written word. Poetry is made of what you hear in language.'
– W S Merwin, *RTE Radio 1*, March 2004

'A poem is very like a prayer: it's shareable; you're talking to something that you don't know is there or not; you don't know if you've got a listener or not; it's a blank page just as heaven is a blank page; and you have this act of faith in poetry, just as you have in a prayer.'
– Brendan Kennelly, *BBC Radio 4*, March 2004

'Register offices in Britain are banning some of the best-loved poems from being read out at weddings because they contain "religious" words.'
– Will Iredale, *The Sunday Times*, 30 May 2004

'People would rather read my prose because they don't know that it's writing – it doesn't bother them. Poetry always says that it's writing.'
– Clive James, *New Straits Times*, 3 March 2004

'Maybe it's just as well nobody reads poetry. If taxpayers knew what their money was being spent on, they'd probably ask for a refund.'
– Eilis O'Hanlon, *The Sunday Independent*, 11 April 2004

'If every person in the country was buying poetry and it was available on every street corner and when you turned on BBC 1 on Saturday night, poetry probably wouldn't be doing its job.'
– Simon Armitage, *The Independent*, 13 March 2004

'If a thing isn't commercial it has a kind of holiness about it which exempts it from responsibility. Poems are chits that get you off work.'
– Hugo Williams, *Times Literary Supplement*, 23 April 2004

'Watch out for our coming campaign, called Get the Poets Back into Banks, Doctors' Surgeries and Insurance Offices, where modern poetry began.'
– James Campbell, *Times Literary Supplement*, 11 June 2004

'On both sides of our family we were workers in iron – and I suppose I like to think I'm a worker in iron also.'
– Geoffrey Hill, *BBC Radio 3*, April 2004

'Writing comes to be associated with the outlaw parts of the self, but one really needs an orderly, bourgeois life to get work done.'
– Robert Hass, *Smartishpace*, 2004

'My experience of poetic ideas is that they don't stand there waiting calmly until you're ready to receive them. You have to rush out and welcome them immediately…'
– Ian Duhig, *The Stinging Fly*, Winter/Spring 2004

'Poetry tells us, at its best, what life – experience, imagination, thought and emotion together – feels like with all its delights, losses, paradoxes and contradictions.'
– George Szirtes, *PBS Bulletin*, Spring 2004

'In the end we go to poetry for one reason, so that we might more fully inhabit our lives and the world in which we live them, and that if we more fully inhabit these things, we might be less apt to destroy both.'
– Christian Wiman, *Poetry*, April 2004

'Poetry…creates a metaphor, which enables the reader to experience what you have experienced with a kind of specificity and depth that is not possible in casual language, partly because the form also communicates the information.'
– Stephen Dobyns, *The Cortland Review*, Spring 2004

'My poems are formal for the simple reason that if they weren't I wouldn't know when to stop.'
– Michael Longley, *PBS Bulletin*, Spring 2004

'He had for the past two decades lived an ascetic existence in Japan, with little interest in winning greater reward for his own poems. Of these, some 80,000 remain unpublished. Until he slipped into a coma on December 31 last year, he was still writing the equivalent of a small book of poetry every day.'
– Obituary of Cid Corman, *The Times*, 29 March 2004

'One female poet comments: "Men, relative to women, often seem to move twice as fast and go twice as far, based on having done about half the amount of work, that is – half the writing, half the schmoozing, half the experience."'
– Suzi Feay, *The Independent*, 7 March 2004

'There seems to be a confidence issue in being a woman poet that is different to men. It's a more difficult identity to claim for yourself, if you're a woman. Being the object of poetry for so many years, women will naturally find it harder than men to be the subject of their work. It's very unfeminine to be a poet.'
– Sarah Maguire, *The Wolf*, April 2004

'A tide is turning in contemporary poetry. More women poets are finding their voices than ever before. The last bastion of literary testosterone is starting to fall.'
– Debbie Taylor, *Mslexia*, January / February 2004

'As a poet in the Irish language, the poetry is vitally important – but it doesn't make any money… I'm tempted more and more to write in English.'
– Cathal Ó Searcaigh, *RTE Radio* 1, March 2004

'The act of translation is an absolutely central part of a culture affirming inclusiveness.'
– Tom Paulin, *RTE Radio* 1, March 2004

'The translator's relation to his to-be-translated writer, or victim, is essentially erotic and an exchange of mental fluids that cannot be entirely justified or explained.'
– Richard Howard, *The Paris Review*, Spring 2004

'Slams are a long way from the older idea of poetry readings, often in a draughty library, where an intense soul in corduroy trousers is whispering his free translations of Rilke's sonnets.'
– Tom Payne, *The Daily Telegraph*, 10 April 2004

'Sooner or later every wannabe versifier will turn up at an open poetry night to vomit spiritually over the other would-be poets in the crowd. And be under no illusion, the entire audience is sitting on a sonnet; there would be no one there otherwise.'
– Patrick Hussey, *The Independent on Sunday*, 18 April 2004

'Writing satire about the poetry world is like shooting similes in a barrel. Line for line, there's no more fertile subject than the black turtleneck crowd clutching their foundation-funded chapbooks in the student lounge.'
– Ron Charles, *Christian Science Monitor*, 20 April 2004

'People always go to poetry when they're deeply distressed. When they fire people from jobs they should give them books of poems.'
– Tony Hoagland, *Houston Chronicle*, 14 February 2004

'People who aren't poets seem to think that, if [great writers] had miserable lives, it was somehow worth it because they wrote these wonderful poems – well I don't. I don't want Emily Dickinson's life, thank you very much...'
– Wendy Cope, *BBC Radio 3*, April 2004

'We are lonely for where we are. Poetry helps us cope.'
– Tim Lilburn, *Poetry International* 7/8, 2003/4

'Poets are basically people that live alone, no matter what else they do.'
– Philip Levine, *Seattle Post-Intelligencer*, 5 March 2004

'Lyric poets / Usually have...cold hearts. / It is like a medical condition. Perfection in art / Is given in exchange for such an affliction.'
– Czeslaw Milosz, *The New Yorker*, 17 May 2004

'Most of the poems I've written to my husband are ambivalent. We had a long and embattled marriage.'
– Elaine Feinstein, quoted in *The Independent,* 27 April 2004

'The California Supreme Court is deciding whether to let stand the criminal conviction of a 15-year-old boy who was expelled from school and served 100 days in juvenile hall for writing a poem that included a threat to kill students.'
– Associated Press Report, *Fox News*, 28 May 2004

'You start from the wrong place with political poetry, because you start by knowing too much, and so what you're likely to write is propaganda.'
– W S Merwin, *The Irish Times*, 20 March 2004

'A poem or short story or novel is not necessarily impelled by the most apocalyptic events available. Sometimes a poem will arise if you just stumble going down the stairs.'
– Denis Donoghue, *RTE Radio* 1, February 2004

'Painful experiences don't easily translate into great, or even adequate, poetry. The validity of the suffering is irrelevant.'
– Alexandra Yurkovsky, *San Francisco Chronicle*, 25 April 2004

'Good literature…doesn't evade any of the terrible things in life. It faces them and faces them squarely, but puts them in a context in which they have a richer meaning than they would as simply raw, descriptive facts.'
– Anthony Hecht, *Humanities*, March/April 2004

'True, Milosevic "manipulated" nationalist passions – but it was writers… who delivered him the stuff to be manipulated… Instead of the industrial-military complex, we in post-Yugoslavia had the poetic-military complex, personified in Radovan Karadzic, the Bosnia-Serb poet-warrior.'
– Slavoj Zizek, *The Guardian*, 1 May 2004

'A great danger we encounter, as poets away from direct participation in the affairs of the community, is that we take ourselves easily as the guardians of moral purity. I can always proclaim: Politics is dirty and the government is corrupt, but I as a poet am clean; my aims are beyond reproach. This… leads to a sort of vanity in the poet, an arrogance.'
– Jayanta Mahapatra, *Contemporary Poetry Review*, April 2004

'For every lie we're told by advertisers and politicians, we need one poem to balance it.'
– Jorie Graham, quoted in *Newsweek*, 12 April 2004

'It is a truth universally acknowledged – at least it should be – that an anthology is a book that omits your favorite poem.'
– Dana Gioia, *Poetry*, April 2004

'To anthologize is to compromise, so the reader of any anthology really needs to know the work well enough to recognize omissions – and their implications. Yet anthologies are aimed at precisely the other kind of reader – one who is relying on the anthology for some guidance, or worse (as in the classroom), relying on it to be definitive.'
– Judith Kitchen, *The Georgia Review*, Winter 2003

'Just as the richest people are the most prone to regard capitalism as even-handed competition, so the most successful poets are the likeliest to assume that the business is a pure meritocracy.'
– Jon Volkmer, *Parnassus*, Vol. 27, Nos. 1 & 2, 2003

'During more than thirty years of observation, I've seen many talents flare only to fizzle out; and some few continue to hold public attention. The readership tends to place its highest hopes on unfamiliar figures, greeting them with a messianic fervor hard to sustain when a second or third book appears.'
– Alfred Corn, *Contemporary Poetry Review*, May 2004

'Too often you get the impression that poets' first books are either their best, or the one in which they satisfied the taste of their time, and that the subsequent work is a gradually diminishing set of variations on the same themes or poses.'
– W N Herbert, *Poetry London*, Spring 2004

'I started writing when I was 28. I don't think people really write anything worth reading before that. You have to be a grown-up to write poetry, and you have to have read quite a lot of poems too.'
– Kate Clanchy, *The Daily Telegraph*, 13 March 2004

'Poets produce twice as much of their lifetime output in their 20s as novelists do. A great novelist or non-fiction writer who dies at 28 may not have yet produced her or his magnum opus.'
– James Kaufman, *The Guardian*, 23 April 2004

'After a certain age, a poet's main rival is the poet he used to be.'
– William Logan, *Parnassus*, Vol. 27, Nos. 1 & 2, 2003

> Relax, Trekkies. To you, it might conjure up an image of Captain Jean-Luc Picard and crew zipping through space at warp factor 5, but the Next Generation I'm referring to are far more terrestrial. They're poets! Twenty of them, to be precise. Their mission – to boldly take poetry to far-flung corners of the universe or, failing that, to give readings at festivals and events throughout the country, advertising the merits of contemporary British poetry and hopefully shifting a few units into the bargain.

So begins Simon Armitage's introduction to the 'Next Generation,' a promotion of twenty British poets chosen by a panel as successors to the 'New Generation' a decade ago. That promotion was a conscious effort to glamorise the perpetually unglamorous, to propel poets into the glare of PR, in the hope, presumably, that the product would catch, and thousands of hitherto untapped consumers enthusiastically consume the product:

> Poetry, apparently, was about to replace stand-up comedy as the new rock'n'roll. Poetry was Britpop. Poetry was New Labour. Poetry was outselling hardback fiction. Poetry was sexy, and suddenly there we were, the 20 newest, poppiest, wittiest, most saleable and sexiest of them all.

Nor was this a random grouping of talents, according to Armitage, but a conscious articulation of a new moment, a new school, a new sensibility and a new hunger for attention.

> We'd lived through Thatcher; we weren't trying to whip up a revolutionary frenzy, but when big-spending city types were swanking about and mouthing off in the wine bars of Docklands, why should we be content to write small, dusty and innocuous poems for an audience of nobody? Alert to shifts in the language, appalled by elitism, empowered by a free education and not at all embarrassed or apologetic about our lack of literary pedigree, we were a School. We had things to say, we were good at saying them, and we wanted to be heard.

It's hard to imagine an equivalent kind of articulation here, maybe because this argument, this tone is so culturally specific to a laddish, Blairite, Cool Britannia vision of poetry. Ireland is in any case too small to sustain the kind of grand literary campaign that anoints a clutch of novelists or poets and dispatches them to the waiting nation. But does this kind of razzmatazz actually work? Does it really raise the profile of poetry, or does it only draw attention to the personalities of the chosen poets? ('Do you think poetry is the new rock'n'roll?' 'What's your favourite word?,' 'When did you start to write?' pant the *Guardian* journalists). Armitage's own cameo of the burdens of fame is hardly mind-expanding:

> .....for reasons that are now unclear to me several of us were asked to dress up like cartoon cat-burglars before being assaulted with a bucket of water. I have a firm memory of telling the man behind the lens to fuck off, but when delivered from a poet standing in a skin-tight polo-neck, Lycra ski-pants and pop socks, I guess the insult doesn't carry much weight. I don't have a lot of advice for the poets of the Next Generation (they're the competition, for God's sake), but here's one tip: when the stuck-for-ideas photographer lifts up the fire extinguisher – duck.

Any promotional exercise necessarily involves simplification; in this case poetry must be packaged as a group of identifiable poets armed with soundbites and photos, and in order to justify the hullabaloo the selection must seem to have judiciously plucked 'the best' from the available contemporary practice. And although Armitage presents the selection, chosen by a panel of seven including himself, a member of Radiohead, and English poet laureate Andrew Motion, as a 'celebration' and simply a selection of what was available, the article's subhead baldly states 'They're Britain's best new poets, chosen... for the verve of their verse' and the surrounding publicity leaves no doubt that these are the pick of the pack. These are the names the journalists, librarians, English teachers and festival organisers will be reaching for, with the poets not on the list inevitably seen as also-rans. (This year's Ledbery festival, a colleague writes, featured an event whose hastily revised title read 'Roddy Lumsden and Next Generation poets,' Roddy Lumsden having committed the awkward blunder of not being chosen). And of course many of those selected are fine poets – Maurice Riordan (awarded honorary Britishness), Gwyneth Lewis, Paul Farley, Alice Oswald to name just a few. Not all of them, incidentally, in this odd configuration of 'generation' are that 'next,' several being older and longer in the poetic tooth than their predecessors in the 'New Generation.' What do the stars of ten years time get called? After 'New' and 'Next,' what next?

But in the end this kind of promotion ends up selling poetry short. It necessarily aligns poetry with the values of marketing, of a world in a hurry which has little time for poetry and therefore must have it pitched at it as briefly and painlessly as possible. The Next Generation doesn't in fact present a range of contemporary practice, or anything like it. It offers no work outside what Don Paterson (see David Wheatley's piece in this issue) would call the 'UK mainstream.' Poets are roped together under a flag of populist chic perfectly embodied by Armitage's breathless prose, and though it may well bring the work of some poets to the wide attention they deserve, it will also serve to narrow the spectrum, the scope of possibility. Big marketing campaigns can only understand poetry in terms of marketing, they turn poetry into a quest for approval where you struggle to get to the top, pushing your 'enemies' aside. You're 'the best' or 'the rest,' baby. Possibly the worst side effect is that it makes poetry all too eager to meet the world on the world's own terms. 'Poets of the Next Generation, don't let us down. The gates of the Chocolate Factory are wide open and waiting for you.' Like, relax, Trekkies.

★★★

After all the excitement above it might come as a relief to some that poetry is, in fact, dying again. The Scottish-American poetry magazine, *The Dark Horse*, for Spring 2004, reprints 'Why Poetry is Dying' an address given by Dr Joesph P Salemi before the New York Poetry Forum at the Soldiers', Sailors', Marines' and Airmen's Club in Manhattan in November 2001. The death of poetry has been proclaimed at regular intervals ever since two words rubbed up against each other in the mouth of a bard beyond in the mists of time. *Poetry? Call that poetry, Homer?* Dr Salemi isolates three primary causes which are causing the death of the art in our own time. First up is quantity: 'There is far too much poetry being written and published. Never before in the history of English literature has so much text been generated by so many self-designated poets.' Then there are the qualitative problems: 'First and foremost, contemporary poetry is crippled by the fact that only one particular rhetorical mode is considered acceptable and prestigious. That mode is the confessional lyric.' Needless to say contemporary poetry means contemporary American poetry, and his example of a typical poetry publication is *The New Yorker*, which makes us think Dr Salemi needs to get out more and visit a few more bookshops. The last problem he diagnoses is what he calls 'Portentous Hush,' which is likely to rise up and strike at any time. What is it? 'Portentous Hush is an atmosphere, a tonality, an attitude. It is the tendency of contemporary verse to generate an air of highfalutin sanctity about itself, to pose before the reader as Something of Great Importance.' In order to avoid overproduction, lyric hegemony and Portentous Hush, Dr Salemi helpfully provides eight rules of which we here give numbers two and five: 'If your language is indistinguishable from common speech, give up poetry'; 'Do not write any poems about your grandchildren, your pet cat, or the natural beauty of the New England Wood.' The Cat Flap offers five euro for the best poem about a lost grandchild and his/her cat of an autumn day in New Hampshire. The issue also contains a vigorous and diverting rebuttal of Dr Salemi's arguments by Philip Hobsbaum. *The Dark Horse*, 16, Spring 2004. Edited by Gerry Cambridge. Editorial addresses: UK: Gerry Cambridge, c/o 3 (b) Blantyre Mill Road, Bothwell, South Lanarkshire G71 8DD; USA: Jennifer Goodrich, 70 Lincoln Avenue, Hastings-on-Hudson, New York 10706. E-mail **gjctdh@freenetname.co.uk**

***

Harold Pinter has been awarded the Wilfred Owen award for poetry for his verses against the invasion of Iraq, an award previously won by Seamus Heaney. According to Michael Grayer, the chairman of the Wilfred Owen Association, the honour is partly in recognition of Pinter's lifelong contribution to literature, 'and specifically for his collection of poetry entitled *War*, published in 2003.' The book consists of a speech, seven poems written immediately before last year's Iraq war, and one poem on the 1991 Gulf war. According to a recent report in *The Guardian*, the association came under pressure from members in the build-up to the war to declare a view on the conflict. It decided against this but its newsletter published many poems, mostly against the war. Under the announcement on Pinter, the newsletter quotes from a *New York Times* article which says: 'The Bush administration has been loudly attacking the news media for misreporting the conflict,' to which it replies 'Owen would counter – in vivid, gripping images – that it is the White House which is dangerously distorting reality.' The most quoted poem on Iraq, and one which has been much vilified by Bush supporters, is 'God Bless America':

> Here they go again
> The Yanks in their armoured parade
> Chanting their ballads of joy
> As they gallop across the big world
> Praising America's God.
> The gutters are clogged with the dead.

***

Verse, Volume 20, Numbers 2 & 3 is now available (Department of English, University of Georgia, Athens, GA 30602, USA), and is a prose issue with prose of various kinds by poets, interviews with, among others, Ed Dorn, Kevin Hart, Charles North, and Don Paterson. Don Paterson is asked what effect the New Generation promotion had on him.

> It wasn't a good thing, though I think it was a good thing in terms of
> PR, it was not very good for poetry as a whole. As far as individual poets
> were concerned, I don't think it did any of them much good at all; it just
> inspired a lot of jealousy. The perception was, at least among the poets

who were left out, that we all got loads of gigs out of it. If we got two each that was about the size of it. And of course there were some members of the public who really thought we were all travelling around in a big bus living in one house like the Monkees. The other downside was that it made everybody really self-conscious about what it was they were doing, and it made them examine it in a way they wouldn't have had to do otherwise. Personally speaking, I don't think it made any difference to poetry, but it didn't make me feel too good.

The issue also contains a slew of reviews of a wide range of critical prose, memoir and poetry. We thought we would leave you with a passage from Christopher Logue's memoir, *Prince Charming*, as quoted in Adam Novy's review. Novy has been discussing Logue's acquaintance with famous people, including Samuel Beckett, Doris Lessing, and 'in the book's incomparable episode, jazz musician Artie Shaw, a friend of a friend who collects him from the airport':

> The maestro switched on the car's internal lights, slid back the driver's seat, took out his penis and said, in a formal voice: 'Christopher, to let you know you are now in the big time, take a look at a prick that has fucked Lana Turner and Ava Gardner.'

★★★

The latest issue of *Southword* reveals the first fruits of an innovative translation venture, the Munster Literature Centre's Cork 2005 translation project, which is part of the programme for Cork's reign as Capital of European Culture. Thirteen Cork-born English-language poets have been commissioned to select a poet from 'thirteen countries on the far side of Europe.' The two stipulations were that the poet must be still living and must not yet have had a book translated into English. 'There is a wide variety of approach among the Irish poets,' says editor and Munster Literature Centre Director Patrick Cotter. 'Many are being as faithful as they can to the original texts, others are exploring the texts' possibilities for being springboards of creativity in English.' The issue also contains new prose from James Lasdun, Desmond Hogan, Hansjörg Schertenlieb and others, and reviews of recent poetry. *Southword* 6, The Munster Literatures Centre, Tigh Litríochta, Frank O'Connor House, 84 Douglas Street, Cork. E-mail: **munsterlit@eircom.net**

Notes on Contributors

Fergus Allen's most recent collection, *Mrs Power Looks Over the Bay*, was published by Faber and Faber in 1999.

Alma Carey-Zúñiga's publications include contributions to *Creating Fiction* (Story Press, 1999) and *State of the Union 2.001* (EMF, 2001). Born in Mexico, she now lives in Wicklow.

Gerald Dawe has published six collections of poetry, including *The Morning Train* (1999) and *Lake Geneva* (2003), both from Gallery. *The Night Fountain: Uncollected Poems of Salvatore Quasimodo*, translated with Marco Sonzogni, is forthcoming from Arc.

Alistair Elliot has translated *Alcestis*, *Oedipus* and *Medea* for the theatre, also books by Heine and Verlaine.

Peter Fallon is a poet and publisher. *The Georgics of Virgil* is published this September, the month his *Tarry Flynn* (also available from Gallery) opens in the United States.

Eamon Grennan's most recent books are *Still Life with Waterfall* (Gallery, 2001) and *Facing the Music: Irish Poetry in the 20th Century* (Creighton University Press, 1999).

Vona Groarke's collections are *Shale* (1994), *Other People's Houses* (1999) and *Flight* (2002), all from Gallery.

Biddy Jenkinson Iar-eagarthóir ar Éigse Éireann. Foilseoidh Coiscéim, *Púca Púca*, leabhar dá cuid do leanaí dána, go luath. Sonas ort a léitheoir.

James J McAuley's tenth collection of poems, *Meditations, With Distractions*, was published by University of Arkansas Press in 2001.

John McAuliffe's first collection is *A Better Life*, published by Gallery in 2002. He lives in Manchester.

Jamie McKendrick's *The Marble Fly* won the Forward Prize for Best Collection in 1997.

Eugenio Montale, who won the 1975 Nobel Prize in Literature, brought the tradition of Italian lyric poetry that begins with Dante into the twentieth century with unrivalled power and brilliance. Jonathan

Galassi's versions of Montale's major work, *Collected Poems* 1920-1954, (Farrar, Strauss and Giroux, 1998) is a useful introduction.

Mary O'Donnell's fourth collection *September Elegies* was published by Lapwing in 2003. She is also a novelist.

Dennis O'Driscoll's *New and Selected Poems,* a Poetry Book Society Special Commendation, will be published by Anvil in October.

Gréagóir Ó Dúill is assistant director of the Poets' House in Falcarragh, and co-ordinator of the M.A. programme there. His *Rogha Dánta* 1965-2001 was published by Coiscéim/Cois Life in 2001.

Ruairí Ó hUiginn is Professor of Modern Irish at Maynooth and editor of *Léachtaí Cholm Cille.* In addition to articles on Old, Middle and Modern Irish, he edited the texts as well as supplying the linguistic commentary in the major two-volume collection of Carna material entitled *Airneán* (1996), and contributed the chapter on present-day Connacht Irish to *Stair na Gaeilge.*

Michael O'Loughlin was born in Dublin in 1958. He publications include the collections *Atlantic Blues* (Raven Arts Press, 1982), *Diary of A Silence* (Raven Arts Press, 1985), *Another Nation: New and Selected Poems* (New Island Press, 1995), a volume of translations from the Dutch, and a critical essay on Patrick Kavanagh entitled *After Kavanagh: Patrick Kavanagh and the Discourse of Contemporary Irish Poetry* (Raven Arts Press, 1985).

Barra Ó Seaghdha is a teacher, editor and critic. He lives in Dublin.

Marcus Perryman was born in England in 1956 and has lived in Italy since 1977. With Peter Robinson he has also published translations of Sereni's prose, and poetry by Ungaretti, Franco Fortini and Maurizio Cucchi.

Adrian Rice is a poet and editor. *The Mason's Tongue* (Abbey Press, 1999) was shortlisted for the 2001 Christopher Ewart-Biggs Memorial Literary Prize and was nominated for the 2001 Irish Times Poetry Prize. His new volume of poetry, *The Moongate Sonnets*, is forthcoming. He is the Visiting Writer-in-Residence at Lenoir-Rhyne College, North Carolina for 2005.

Peter Robinson's *Selected Poems* was published by Carcanet in 2003.

Aidan Rooney lives in Hingham, Massachusetts and teaches at Thayer Academy. His first collection of poems – *Day Release* – appeared from The Gallery Press in 2000.

Gavin Selerie was born in London in 1949. His published works include *Azimuth* (Binnacle Press, 1984), *Roxy* (West House Books, 1996) and – with Alan Halsey – *Days of '49* (West House Books, 1999). Texts can also be found in *The New British Poetry* (1988), *Ten British Poets* (1993) and *Other: British and Irish Poetry since 1970* (1989). *Le Fanu's Ghost* will be published by Five Seasons Press, Hereford. Further is available from the British Electronic Poetry Centre [**www.soton.ac.uk/–poetry**].

Marco Sonzogni is Faculty Fellow in Italian at University College Dublin and the editor of *Translation Ireland*. He is currently editing *Corno inglese*, an anthology of Eugenio Montale's poetry in English translation. *The Night Fountain*, a selection of Salvatore Quasimodo's early poetry, translated into English with Gerald Dawe, is forthcoming from Arc.

Deborah Tyler-Bennett is a published poet and short fiction writer. Her first volume of poetry, *Clark Gable in Mansfield*, is published by the King's England Press (Rotherham, 2003).

Myra Vennard is a member of Queen's University Belfast Writers' Group. Her publications include reviews and poems in *Fortnight, Poetry Ireland Review, The Honest Ulsterman* and *An Anthology of New Writing from Queen's University*.

David Wheatley edited the *Poems of James Clarence Mangan* for Gallery Press in 2003. His own collections, also from Gallery, are *Thirst* (1997) and *Misery Hill* (2000).

THE POETRY TRUST

16th ALDEBURGH POETRY FESTIVAL
5 — 7 NOVEMBER 2004

The UK's leading annual international celebration of contemporary poetry

A brilliant mix of 30 poets including

MARGARET ATWOOD
HANS MAGNUS ENZENSBERGER
MICHAEL LONGLEY
SARAH MAGUIRE
PAUL MULDOON
MICHAEL ROSEN

advance booking essential

www.thepoetrytrust.org
THE COMPLETE POETRY WEEKEND